We the People

An Introduction to
American Politics

TEST-ITEM FILE

We the People

An Introduction to American Politics

FOURTH EDITION

Douglas Dow
THE UNIVERSITY OF TEXAS AT DALLAS

 W • W • NORTON & COMPANY • NEW YORK • LONDON

Copyright © 2003, 2001, 1999, 1997 by W. W. Norton & Company, Inc.

All rights reserved.

Printed in the United States of America.

Composition and layout by Roberta Flechner Graphics.

ISBN 0-393-97976-8

W. W. Norton & Company, Inc., 500 Fifth Avenue, New York, NY 10110
www.wwnorton.com

W. W. Norton & Company Ltd., Castle House, 75/76 Wells Street, London W1T 3QT

1 2 3 4 5 6 7 8 9 0

CONTENTS

Chapter 1 | American Political Culture — 1

Chapter 2 | The Founding and the Constitution — 12

Chapter 3 | Federalism — 25

Chapter 4 | Civil Liberties — 37

Chapter 5 | Civil Rights — 52

Chapter 6 | Public Opinion — 67

Chapter 7 | The Media — 80

Chapter 8 | Political Participation and Voting — 92

Chapter 9 | Political Parties — 104

Chapter 10 | Campaigns and Elections — 118

Chapter 11 | Groups and Interests — 130

Chapter 12 | Congress — 144

Chapter 13 | The Presidency — 160

Chapter 14 | Bureaucracy in a Democracy — 173

Chapter 15 | The Federal Courts — 185

Chapter 16 | Government and the Economy — 197

Chapter 17 | Social Policy — 209

Chapter 18 | Foreign Policy — 220

TEXAS EDITION

Chapter 19 | The Political Culture, People, and Economy of Texas   232

Chapter 20 | The Texas Constitution   238

Chapter 21 | Parties and Elections in Texas   245

Chapter 22 | Interest Groups, Lobbying, and Lobbyists in Texas   251

Chapter 23 | The Texas Legislature   257

Chapter 24 | The Texas Executive Branch   263

Chapter 25 | The Texas Judiciary   269

Chapter 26 | Local Government in Texas   276

Chapter 27 | Public Policy in Texas   282

CHAPTER 1 | American Political Culture

MULTIPLE CHOICE

1. Since the 1960s, Americans' trust in their government generally has
   A. remained fairly stable.
   B. risen slightly.
   C. fallen slightly.
   D. fallen sharply.

   D (p. 7)

2. Which of the following is NOT a consequence of the decline in trust toward government?
   A. The government is unable to attract good workers into the public sector.
   B. People are less willing to pay the taxes necessary for public activities.
   C. Distrust weakens government's ability to help people in times of crisis.
   D. All of the above are consequences of a decline in trust.

   D (p. 11)

3. The belief that you can influence how your government acts is called
   A. political efficacy.
   B. saliency.
   C. popular sovereignty.
   D. autocracy.

   A (p. 12)

4. The decline of political efficacy results from
   A. the belief that citizens cannot effect what happens in government.
   B. the decline in active participation in public debates.
   C. the decline in political knowledge.
   D. All of the above.

   D (p. 12)

5. Which of the following is NOT a reason given to explain the increased apathy in American citizens?
   A. a decline in citizens' understanding about politics
   B. the increasing belief that people cannot make a difference in politics
   C. an increase in the knowledge about how government operates
   D. the perception that government is out of touch with public opinion

   C (pp. 12, 14)

6. In order to be a good citizen, it is most critical to possess
   A. powerful friends.
   B. money.
   C. knowledge.
   D. strongly held convictions.

   C (p. 14)

7. Survey data shows that the level of Americans' political knowledge is
   A. uniformly high.
   B. distressingly low.
   C. high regarding history but low regarding governmental processes.
   D. High concerning current events but low concerning historical facts.

   B (p. 14)

8. According to the textbook, which of the following is the most important act of a citizen?
   A. participating in public debates
   B. voting for the candidate of one's choice
   C. holding office in the government
   D. being born in the nation of which you are a citizen

   A (p. 15)

9. Which of the following is NOT a necessary part of the knowledge a citizen needs to have?
   A. the structures of government
   B. the political process
   C. democratic principles
   D. the economic interests of other citizens

   D (p. 15)

10. Why might Adam Smith's idea of the "invisible hand" not apply well to government?
    A. The government is neither rational nor cost effective.
    B. Not all of government's goals can be solved through individual action.
    C. The need for transparency means that nothing in government can be invisible.
    D. According to the text, the invisible hand is a good metaphor for government.

    B (p. 16)

11. What is the principle difference between an autocracy and an oligarchy?
    A. the responsiveness to popular opinion
    B. the number of people in charge
    C. the level of wealth of the rulers
    D. international diplomatic recognition

    B (p. 17)

12. An autocracy exists when
    A. the government is controlled by a single individual.
    B. the government is controlled by a small but powerful group of people.
    C. the constitution of a government is strictly followed.
    D. government is controlled by one dominant religious group.

    A (p. 17)

13. Government can best be defined as
    A. the institutions and procedures by which a piece of territory and its people are ruled.
    B. the set of political principles and values that guide political life.
    C. the legalized theft of others property.
    D. the invisible hand that turns private interests into public goods.

    A (p. 16)

14. A service that a person needs but is usually unable to provide for him- or herself individually is called
    A. a public good.
    B. a cultural commodity.
    C. an oligarchy.
    D. an entitlement

    A (p. 16)

15. Which of the following is NOT an example of a public good?
    A. a military defense force
    B. a police force
    C. a job
    D. the administration of the courts

    C (p. 17)

16. Which of the following is NOT an example given by the textbook of a totalitarian regime?
    A. pre–World War II Italy
    B. the Soviet Union
    C. Nazi Germany
    D. the United Kingdom

    D (p. 17)

17. Before the eighteenth century,
    A. governments were primarily democratic.
    B. totalitarian rule was common.
    C. governments rarely sought the support of their people.
    D. most governments were based on respect for the rule of law.

    C (p. 17)

18. According to the textbook, what is the main benefit of a constitutional government?
    A. The government is limited by the rule of law.
    B. The government must obey democracy.
    C. The government will distribute social goods equally.
    D. The government is stable.

    A (p. 17)

19. What are the two major changes that occurred in Western governments that led to the establishment of a constitutional government?
    A. legal limits on government and the right of more people to vote
    B. the right of revolution and the spread of socialism
    C. debt relief for the poor and the right of subjects to hold office
    D. the colonialism of the New World and the right of revolution

    A (p. 17)

20. A government that is formally limited by laws and rules is called
    A. democratic.
    B. constitutional.
    C. oligarchic.
    D. authoritarian.

    B (p. 17)

21. The demand during the American Revolution for no taxation without representation is a good example of what political reform of the eighteenth century?
    A. more popular influence on government
    B. the decline in citizenship
    C. the spread of autocracy
    D. greater attention to the economic effects of politics

    A (p. 18)

22. The key group in Europe that pushed for limited government was
    A. the bourgeoisie.
    B. the *idiotes*.
    C. the citizens.
    D. the poor.

    A (p. 18)

23. Why did the Progressives support women's suffrage in the early twentieth century?
    A. The Progressives were a group dominated by women.
    B. The Progressives wanted to make the United States as democratic as possible.
    C. The Progressives believed women would support their reform movement.
    D. The Progressives needed to develop a voting bloc to check and limit upper-middle-class northerners.

    C (p. 19)

24. Who described politics as "who gets what, when, and how"?
    A. James Madison
    B. Abraham Lincoln
    C. Harold Lasswell
    D. Franklin Roosevelt

    C (p. 19)

25. According to the textbook, what is the goal of politics?
    A. to have a say in a government's leadership, organization, and policies
    B. to get as much power as possible in order to serve one's own interests
    C. to construct a perfect constitutional order
    D. to construct a political system conducive to economic growth

    A (p. 19)

26. Direct democracy is best defined as
    A. a state of continual revolution.
    B. the system that allows people to vote by telephone or over the Internet.
    C. a system that allows citizens to vote directly for laws and policies.
    D. the competition between interest groups for governmental power.

    C (p. 19)

27. Having some share or say in the composition of a government's leadership, how government is organized, or what its policies are going to be is called
    A. government.
    B. power
    C. autocracy.
    D. federalism.

    B (p. 19)

28. The struggle of competing interest groups for governmental influence is called
    A. pluralism.
    B. direct action politics.
    C. direct democracy.
    D. oligarchy.

    A (p. 19)

29. According to the textbook, which of the following is NOT one of the core American political values?
    A. liberty
    B. equality
    C. democracy
    D. socialism

    D (p. 20)

30. The Bill of Rights is
    A. the first ten amendments to the Constitution.
    B. the first constitution the United States wrote.
    C. the charter of freedom established by the English lords against the King.
    D. the Fourteenth Amendment.

    A (p. 21)

31. The Bill of Rights was designed to protect
    A. equality.
    B. liberty.
    C. democracy.
    D. All of the above.

    B (p. 21)

32. What are the three core values of American politics?
    A. liberty, equality, and democracy
    B. democracy, patriotism, and the rule of law
    C. equality, oligarchy, and free enterprise
    D. anarchy, equality, and patriotism

    A (p. 20)

33. In American political culture, economic freedom means
    A. low inflation.
    B. job security.
    C. laissez-faire capitalism.
    D. low taxes.

    C (p. 21)

34. The right of each citizen to vote is an example of
    A. equality of opportunity.
    B. equality of result.
    C. political equality.
    D. educational opportunity.

    C (p. 22)

35. "One person, one vote" reflects the principle of
    A. political equality.
    B. equality of opportunity.
    C. majority rule.
    D. economic liberty.

    A (p. 22)

36. The belief that political authority should rest with the people themselves is called
    A. equality of opportunity.
    B. political equality.
    C. pluralism.
    D. popular sovereignty.

    D (p. 24)

37. Affirmative action is very controversial because
    A. Americans argue about whether it promotes or restrains equality.
    B. it is inherently an undemocratic way of achieving liberty.
    C. some argue that it limits political equality in order to promote cost effectiveness.
    D. it is a legacy of the Jim Crow years.

    A (p. 27)

8 | Chapter 1

38. Which of the following statements concerning political values in the United States is true?
    A. American values often conflict with each other in practice.
    B. Because of their diversity, Americans do not share a similar set of core political values.
    C. The origins of American political values are found in the 1960s.
    D. American politics relies on its value neutrality.

    A (p. 24)

39. Political rights are a protection against
    A. pluralism.
    B. the tyranny of the majority.
    C. the equality of result.
    D. socialism.

    B (p. 24)

40. What is the most important check on majority rule in the United States?
    A. popular sovereignty
    B. pluralism
    C. minority rights
    D. laissez-faire

    C (p. 24)

41. Approximately what percentage of the world population lives in nations considered free?
    A. 15 percent
    B. 25 percent
    C. 40 percent
    D. 65 percent

    C (p. 25)

42. The existence of slavery in the United States is a good example of how
    A. American values are not always reflected in practice.
    B. Americans do not value liberty.
    C. European ideals have influenced American political culture.
    D. political needs are often placed above economic needs.

    A (pp. 25–26)

43. The separate but equal doctrine was introduced in what Supreme Court case?
    A. *Plessy v. Ferguson*
    B. the Civil Rights Cases
    C. *Brown v. Board of Education*
    D. *Roe v. Wade*

    A (p. 27)

44. Disputes over affirmative action demonstrate that
    A. Americans disagree over what is the public's legitimate role in ensuring the equality of opportunity.
    B. Americans are generally supportive of equality of results.
    C. economic liberties are more important than democracy.
    D. Americans have stopped valuing democracy.

    A (p. 27)

45. Which of the following statements is true?
    A. The United States has the greater gap in income between the poorest and richest than any other developed nation.
    B. The gap between the rich and the poor can be explained by an American support of oligarchy.
    C. American politics is structured by centuries-long class antagonism.
    D. Income gaps between Americans are small, compared with those in other developed nations.

    A (p. 29)

46. Which of the following was NOT once a restriction placed on the right to vote?
    A. race
    B. gender
    C. property
    D. All of the above were restrictions.

    D (p. 29)

47. According to the textbook, the United States did not become a fully democratic nation until
    A. the 1860s, after the Civil War.
    B. the 1820s, when property requirements for voting were dropped.
    C. the early twentieth century, when women were granted the suffrage.
    D. the 1960s, when the right of African Americans to vote was enforced by federal laws.

    D (p. 29)

48. Low voter turnout and political apathy endangers
    A. equality.
    B. economic liberty.
    C. democracy.
    D. constitutionalism.

    C (p. 30)

49. Political apathy among Americans hurt which core political value the most?
    A. democracy
    B. freedom of religion
    C. economic liberty
    D. equality of opportunity

    A (p. 30)

50. "Politics" can be defined as
    A. conflicts over the character, membership, and policies of any organization to which people belong.
    B. the informal, private organizations through which a land and its people are ruled.
    C. a hierarchically structured organization that is designed to distribute labor among several different groups of people.
    D. a line-and-staff organization that is designed to facilitate control over complex social arrangements.

    A (p. 19)

51. A representative democracy is a system of government that
    A. allows citizens to vote directly on laws and policies.
    B. allows citizens to personally make, veto, or judge statutes.
    C. gives citizens a regular opportunity to elect top government officials.
    D. gives citizens the ability to make important military decisions directly.

    C (p. 19)

52. "Political culture" refers to the
    A. way that artists, musicians, filmmakers, and cultural critics use their message to influence political decision-making.
    B. factors that influence the way informal social organizations make decisions.
    C. shared values, beliefs, and attitudes that serve to hold a nation and its people together.
    D. way of organizing politically which is defined in the Articles of Confederation.

    C (p. 20)

53. Throughout American history, the concept of liberty has been linked to the
    A. idea of privacy.
    B. idea of limited government.
    C. idea of unlimited government.
    D. Articles of Confederation.

    B (p. 21)

54. The central historical conflict regarding liberty in the United States was the
    A. enslavement of African Americans.

B. granting of the vote to women.
  C. treatment of Native Americans.
  D. treatment of Roman Catholics.

  A (p. 25)

55. Most Americans support the ideal of equality of
    A. result.
    B. opportunity.
    C. process.
    D. the masses.

    B (p. 21)

TRUE OR FALSE

1. Over the past several decades, the public's belief that government is responsive to the people has declined.

   T (p. 12)

2. The most important thing for a citizen to possess is political knowledge.

   T (p. 15)

3. When a single ruler controls all government power, it is called an oligarchy.

   F (p. 17)

4. Constitutional democracies were often found throughout ancient Greece.

   F (p. 17)

5. The proletariat was the key social force leading to limited government during the eighteenth century.

   F (p. 18)

6. The referendum is a form of direct democracy.

   T (p. 19)

7. Because of the diversity of races, ethnicities, and religions, Americans do not share a common political culture.

   F (p. 20)

8. "One person, one vote" summarizes the principle of equality of opportunity.

   F (p. 22)

9. The United States has never accepted the principle of popular sovereignty.

   F (p. 24)

10. Many of the most critical dilemmas of American politics involve conflicts in how commonly held values are put into practice.

    T (p. 30)

CHAPTER 2 | The Founding and the Constitution

MULTIPLE CHOICE

1. What was the primary goal of the Constitution's framers?
   A. to create an effective government
   B. to develop political virtue amongst the citizens
   C. to create a constitution system which would last for centuries
   D. to create a document that made state constitutions unnecessary

   A (p. 38)

2. Which of the following sectors of society did not have interests that were a direct spark for the American Revolution?
   A. New England merchants
   B. Small farmers
   C. Slaves
   D. Royalists loyal to Britain

   C (p. 39)

3. Colonial protesters of the Stamp Act and the Sugar Act rallied around what famous political slogan?
   A. "No taxation without representation."
   B. "Give me liberty or give me death."
   C. "Remember the Alamo."
   D. "A house divided against itself cannot stand."

   A (p. 40)

4. Who defended in court the British soldiers involved in the Boston Massacre?
   A. Thomas Jefferson
   B. Samuel Adams
   C. John Adams
   D. John Hancock

   C (p. 40)

5. The events that lead to the Revolutionary War were sparked by what event?
   A. The British raised revenue by increasing the tax rate of the colonies.
   B. The British had established suspicious alliances with Indian tribes during the French and Indian Wars.
   C. King George II was assassinated by American separatists.
   D. Protestant fundamentalists in New England were attempting to establish a theocracy.

   A (pp. 39–40)

6. What was the most common form of taxation during the colonial era?
   A. income tax
   B. taxes on commercial products and activities
   C. animal head tax
   D. taxes for use of governmental services and lands

   B (p. 39)

7. The Boston Tea Party resulted in all of the following events EXCEPT
   A. the closure of Boston harbor by the British.
   B. the restriction on movement of colonialists to the west.
   C. a change in colonial government.
   D. the Boston Massacre.

   D (pp. 41–42)

8. Which of the following was NOT appointed to help draft the Declaration of Independence?
   A. Thomas Jefferson
   B. Benjamin Franklin
   C. John Adams
   D. George Washington

   D (p. 42)

9. The first written constitution for the United States was called
   A. Magna Carta.
   B. the Bill of Rights.
   C. the Articles of Confederation.
   D. the Constitution.

   C (p. 42)

10. Under the United States's first constitution,
    A. there was no president.
    B. the president was more powerful than Congress.
    C. the Senate was the most powerful political institution.
    D. the president was directly appointed by the state legislatures.

    A (p. 42)

11. How was power in Congress divided under the Articles of Confederation?
    A. Each state had an equal vote.
    B. Each state's votes were proportionate to their population.
    C. The states were not formally represented in Congress.
    D. Each state's power depended on its geographic size.

    A (p. 42)

12. Under the Articles of Confederation, the relationship between the states and the federal government can be best compared to
    A. the United Nations's relationship with member states.
    B. state government's relationship with counties.
    C. state government's relationship with cities.
    D. the Union of Soviet Socialist Republics's relationship with member republics.

    A (p. 43)

13. What was the purpose of the Annapolis Convention?
    A. to discuss the weaknesses of the Articles of Confederation
    B. to plot the revolt known as Shays's Rebellion
    C. to write the Declaration of Independence
    D. to draft a new Bill of Rights

    A (p. 44)

14. A conference held to analyze perceived flaws in the Articles of Confederation was called the
    A. Annapolis Convention.
    B. Philadelphia Convention.
    C. Boston Massacre.
    D. Philadelphia Story.

    A (p. 44)

15. Shays's Rebellion was an attempt to
    A. prevent the state of Massachusetts from foreclosing on the lands of debt ridden farmers.
    B. invade New England by Loyalists from Canada.
    C. overthrow the federal government under the Articles of Confederation.
    D. lead a slave revolt that had spread from Georgia to Virginia.

    A (p. 44)

16. The 1787 convention to draft a new constitution was held in
    A. Boston.
    B. New York City.
    C. Philadelphia.
    D. Washington, D.C.

    C (p. 45)

17. Which was the only state NOT to send delegates to the Constitutional Convention?
    A. Rhode Island
    B. Massachusetts
    C. Virginia
    D. California

    A (p. 44)

18. According to historian Charles Beard, the framers of the Constitution were most concerned with
    A. establishing principles of good government.
    B. pursuing military glory and imperialism.
    C. promoting their economic interests.
    D. creating a religious community.

    C (p. 45)

19. According to the textbook, the writing of the Constitution demonstrates
    A. the marriage of interests and principles.
    B. the triumph of self interest over the common good.
    C. the epitome of civic virtue.
    D. the rupture with the past.

    A (p. 45)

20. The plan at the Constitutional Convention to create a Congress where representation was distributed according to population was called the
    A. Virginia Plan.
    B. Adams Proposal.
    C. New Hampshire Suggestion.
    D. Washington Doctrine.

    A (p. 46)

21. What did the New Jersey Plan propose for Congress?
    A. Representation would be equal for each state.
    B. Representation would be apportioned according to population.
    C. The powers of Congress would check those of state legislatures.
    D. Representatives to Congress would be appointed by the state legislatures.

    A (p. 47)

22. The Great Compromise lead to
    A. the legalization of slavery.
    B. the creation of a bicameral Congress.
    C. the creation of the Supreme Court.
    D. the peaceful conclusion of Shays's Rebellion.

    B (p. 47)

23. James Madison believed that, in the Constitutional Convention, the greatest conflict of interests was revealed to be between
    A. large states and small states.
    B. northern states and southern states.
    C. the wealthy and the poor.
    D. Catholics and Protestants.

    B (p. 48)

24. What is the Three-fifths Compromise?
    A. It determined that three out of every five slaves would be counted for purposes of representation and taxation.
    B. It determined the ratio between free states and slave states.
    C. It created a bicameral legislature.
    D. It declared that the states would pay three-fifths of the Revolutionary War debt and the federal government would pay the rest.

    A (p. 48)

25. Which of the following was a ramification of the Three-fifths Compromise?
    A. It temporarily mended the conflict between northern merchants and southern planters.
    B. It allowed for a political agreement between the North and the South.
    C. It meant that the Constitution officially supported slavery.
    D. All of the above.

    D (pp. 48–49)

26. The ability of the president to veto a bill passed by Congress is a good example of what principle of limited government?
    A. separation of powers
    B. federalism
    C. checks and balances
    D. civil liberties

    C (p. 50)

27. The framers of the Constitution attempted to create an government that could do all of the following EXCEPT
    A. promote commerce and protect private property.
    B. limit excessive democracy.
    C. restrict the power of the central government.
    D. lead to the eventual inclusion of nonwhites into political life.

    D (p. 50)

28. The system of shared powers, divided between a central government and the states, is called
    A. the electoral college.
    B. federalism.
    C. statism.
    D. checks and balances.

    B (p. 50)

29. Which of the following was designed by the framers to be an office directly elected by the people?
    A. congressional representative
    B. senator
    C. president
    D. All of the above.

    A (p. 50)

30. What is the term length of a member of the House of Representatives?
    A. one year
    B. two years
    C. four years
    D. six years

    B (p. 50)

31. Which of the following was NOT a way the framers tried to make the Senate a check against excessive democracy?
    A. The Senate has longer terms than any other federal official.
    B. The Senate has staggered terms of office.
    C. The senators were elected by the state legislatures.
    D. Senators are the only officials immune from impeachment.

    D (pp. 50–51)

32. The powers of Congress under the Constitution are _____ those of Congress under the Articles of Confederation.
    A. greater than
    B. weaker than
    C. similar to
    D. There was no Congress under the Articles of Confederation.

    A (p. 51)

33. The principle of granting the federal government only those powers specifically listed in the Constitution is called
    A. the doctrine of expressed powers.
    B. the theory of separated powers.
    C. civil libertarianism.
    D. autocracy.

    A (p. 51)

34. All of the following are constitutional powers of the president EXCEPT the power to
    A. officially recognize other nations.
    B. grant pardons.
    C. veto bills.
    D. regulate commerce between the states.

    D (p. 51)

35. Alexander Hamilton argued that the chief executive office should possess
    A. popularity.
    B. judgment.
    C. energy.
    D. *gravitas*.

    C (p. 53)

36. The three branches of the government created by the Constitution are
    A. constitutional, elected, and appointed.
    B. executive, legislative, and judicial.
    C. federal, state, and local.
    D. military, courts, and bureaucracy.

    B (pp. 50–53)

37. Judicial review is the power of
    A. the courts to decide on the constitutionality of actions taken by the other branches of government.
    B. Congress to review the decisions of the federal courts.
    C. the president to appoint judges to the federal courts.
    D. the states to review the constitutionality of federal actions and laws.

    A (p. 53)

38. What is the term length of a federal judge?
    A. two years
    B. four years
    C. six years
    D. barring impeachment, for life

    D (p. 53)

39. The supremacy clause
    A. states that Congress is the most powerful branch of the government.
    B. establishes that no branch of government is supreme over others.
    C. announces that the Constitution and all laws made under it are superior to any state laws.
    D. declares that no European powers shall interfere in North America.

    C (p. 54)

40. During the ratification debates, who were the anti-Federalists?
    A. Those who opposed the new Constitution because they wanted a weaker central government.
    B. Those who opposed the Constitution because it did not create a strong enough central government.
    C. Those who supported the Constitution.
    D. Those who believed that the United States should enter into a confederation with Britain and Canada.

    A (p. 58)

41. Which of the following was not one of the writers of the Federalist Papers?
    A. James Madison
    B. John Adams
    C. Alexander Hamilton
    D. John Jay

    B (p. 58)

42. On the subject of representation, anti-Federalists wanted
    A. representative bodies that resembled those represented to the highest degree possible.
    B. representatives to exercise independent judgment and wisdom.
    C. representatives who would reflect commercial interests.
    D. as few representatives as possible.

    A (p. 62)

43. The Federalists believed that the most likely source of tyranny was
    A. the King of Great Britain.
    B. the popular majority.
    C. the northern merchants.
    D. George Washington.

    B (p. 63)

44. The essential dilemma of limited government raised by the ratification debates is
    A. that government too weak to do harm also cannot do good.
    B. power sharing is inherently unstable and too often violent.
    C. a government of expressed powers will slip into an oligarchy.
    D. government may promote civil virtue only at the expense of national power.

    A (p. 65)

45. How many amendments are there to the U.S. Constitution?
    A. ten
    B. twenty
    C. twenty-seven
    D. thirty-three

    C (p. 66)

46. How many proposed amendments to the Constitution have been formally offered to Congress?
    A. fewer than 100
    B. between 100 and 200
    C. between 1,000 and 1500
    D. over 11,000

    D (p. 66)

47. The most common method of passing an amendment to the Constitution is
    A. passage in both houses Congress by a 2/3 vote, followed by a majority vote in 3/4 of the state legislatures.
    B. passage in both houses of Congress by a 2/3 vote, followed by ratification by 3/4 of the state supreme courts.
    C. proposal by the president, which is supported by 2/3 of the state legislatures.
    D. passage by a constitutional convention, called by 3/4 of the states.

    A (p. 67)

48. Why did the Equal Rights Amendment fail to pass?
    A. It was declared unconstitutional by the Supreme Court.
    B. It did not receive enough votes in Congress.
    C. The president vetoed it.
    D. It failed to get the approval of enough state legislatures.

    D (p. 68)

49. Successful amendments to the Constitution
    A. usually are responses to particular topical problems.
    B. are most commonly concerned with the structure or composition of the government.
    C. have often been used to restrict the rights of citizens.
    D. have typically made little effect in the actual working of government.

    B (p. 72)

50. The most important political value for the framers of the Constitution was
    A. democracy.
    B. equality.
    C. liberty.
    D. civic virtue.

    C (p. 74)

51. As a constitution, the Articles of Confederation were concerned primarily with
    A. creating a national government that had significant power and authority.
    B. creating a federal form of government.
    C. creating a form of government in which the states were largely subservient to the national government.
    D. limiting the powers of the central government.

    D (p. 42)

52. Under the Articles of Confederation, it was left to the _____ to execute the laws passed by Congress.
    A. states
    B. chief executive
    C. courts
    D. bureaucracy

    A (p. 42)

53. Shays's Rebellion was significant because it
    A. convinced many observers that the government of the Confederation had become dangerously inefficient and indecisive.
    B. led to the admission of Vermont into the Union.
    C. led to the abolition of slavery.
    D. convinced Congress to approve the Louisiana Purchase.

    A (p. 44)

54. The Virginia Plan of the Constitutional Convention proposed a system of representation in the national legislature that was based upon
    A. equal representation between the states.
    B. the concept of universal suffrage.
    C. the population of each state or the proportion of each state's revenue contribution, or both.
    D. the geographical size of a state.

    C (p. 46)

55. The issue of representation, which threatened to wreck the entire Constitutional Convention, was resolved by the Great Compromise or the
    A. New Jersey Plan.
    B. Connecticut Compromise.
    C. Pennsylvania Compromise.
    D. Virginia Plan.

    B (p. 47)

56. "Bicameralism" is a constitutional principle that means
    A. division of national government into two branches.
    B. division of the powers of the executive branch between two individuals: the president and vice president.
    C. division of the powers of the executive branch between two individuals: the head of state and the head of government.
    D. division of Congress into two chambers.

    D (p. 48)

57. The specific powers granted to Congress by the U.S. Constitution can be found in
    A. Article I, Section 8.
    B. Article II, Section 4.
    C. Article III, Section 5.
    D. the First Amendment.

    A (p. 51)

58. The framers of the Constitution intended to create a presidency capable of
    A. completely dominating Congress.
    B. withstanding excessive popular pressure by making it subject to indirect election through the electoral college.
    C. spending money with little interference from any other branch of government.
    D. regulating all forms of commerce.

    B (p. 53)

59. The concept of separation of powers, as developed in Articles I, II, and III of the U.S. Constitution, includes provision for
    A. three branches of government, a different way of selecting the top personnel of each branch, and a system of checks and balances.
    B. four branches of government, a system of checks and balances, and shared authority over the government's means of coercion.
    C. a bicameral legislative branch and a multiperson executive.
    D. a bicameral legislative branch, an executive branch consisting of a head of state and a head of government, and a Committee of the States.

    A (p. 50)

60. In the national debate over ratification of the new Constitution, the Federalists
    A. supported a return to the Articles of Confederation.
    B. opposed the Constitution and preferred decentralized government.
    C. supported the Constitution and preferred a strong national government.
    D. supported a return to British rule.

    C (p. 58)

61. The Antifederalists' fear of tyranny stemmed from their concern that
    A. the features of the U.S. Constitution which divorced governmental institutions from direct responsibility to the people would lead to a government where a few individuals would use their stations to gain increasing power over the citizenry.
    B. a popular majority would trample the rights of other citizens.
    C. the executive branch possessed entirely too much control of the government's means of coercion.
    D. the Constitution created a system of federal courts that was too extensive and powerful.

    A (p. 63)

62. The Antifederalists argued that the powers of government should be limited by
    A. providing Congress with a larger grant of powers.
    B. decreasing the powers of the executive branch, especially those of the vice president.
    C. confining the powers of the federal government to certain narrowly defined areas and by adding a bill of rights to the Constitution.
    D. creating an internal system of checks and controls within government.

    C (p. 63)

63. The Federalists believed that the powers of government could be limited by
    A. providing Congress with a larger grant of powers.
    B. decreasing the powers of the executive branch, especially those of the vice president.
    C. confining the powers of the federal government to certain narrowly defined areas and by adding a bill of rights to the Constitution.
    D. creating an internal system of checks and controls within government.

    D (p. 63)

TRUE OR FALSE

1. The Declaration of Independence was the United States's first governing constitution.
   F (p. 42)

2. The Articles of Confederation created a weak central government and a loose alliance of nearly independent states.
   T (p. 42)

3. The Great Compromise resulted in a bicameral Congress.
   T (pp. 47–48)

4. The Three-fifths Compromise stated that no more than three out of every five states could be slave states.
   F (p. 48)

5. The doctrine of expressed powers means that Congress does not have any powers not listed in the Constitution.
   T (p. 51)

6. The office of the president was designed by the framers to be capable of energy.
   T (p. 53)

7. The Constitution expressly gave the Supreme Court the power of judicial review over Congress and the president.
   F (p. 53)

8. The anti-Federalists wanted a stronger central government than that proposed in the Constitution.
   F (p. 58)

9. The Federalists believed that the threat of tyranny was most likely to be found in the popular majorities, rather than in a handful of aristocratic persons.
   T (p. 63)

10. The Constitution is a very difficult document to change by amendment.
    T (p. 73)

CHAPTER 3 | Federalism

MULTIPLE CHOICE

1. The vast majority of governmental responsibilities are
   A. the sole responsibility of the federal government.
   B. under the complete authority of state government.
   C. shared by both state and federal authorities.
   D. provided by local government agencies.

   C (p. 81)

2. Over the course of American history, the federal government has grown _____ compared with the states.
   A. stronger
   B. weaker
   C. more expensive
   D. in tandem

   A (p. 82)

3. Which of the following is the best example of a unitary system of government?
   A. The federal government sets education policy for all schools.
   B. The federal government establishes general guidelines for school policy.
   C. The government makes funding for school dependent on test scores.
   D. The federal government gives vouchers to parents for use in private schools.

   A (p. 84)

4. Which of the following nations does NOT have a strong federal system?
   A. Canada
   B. The United States
   C. France
   D. Switzerland

   C (p. 84)

5. The federal system can best be defined as
   A. a system of government where member nations meet in a multinational conference.
   B. a system of government in which power is divided between a national government and lower levels of government.
   C. a system in which the power of the central government is funded through taxation of local government.
   D. the sharing of legislative powers between an upper and lower house.

   B (p. 84)

6. Which of the following is an example of the police powers of state government?
   A. the establishment and funding of a system of criminal law
   B. the regulation of the heath codes
   C. laws establishing curfews
   D. all of the above

   D (p. 85)

7. What is the purpose of the Tenth Amendment?
   A. to give each state constitution the same protections as the federal constitution
   B. to limit the powers of the central government by establishing reserved powers for states and individuals
   C. to grant to the citizens of each state access to the federal court system
   D. to establish the electoral college

   B (p. 84)

8. When both state and national governments possess a certain authority, it is called
   A. an implied power.
   B. a reserved power.
   C. an express power.
   D. a concurrent power.

   D (p. 85)

9. Which of the following is the best example of concurrent powers under the federal constitution?
   A. the power to declare war
   B. the power to coin money
   C. the power to regulate commercial activity
   D. the power to impeach federal officials

   C (p. 85)

10. What constitutional clause affirms that national laws and treaties, made under the authority of the Constitution, are the supreme law of the land?
    A. the full faith and credit clause
    B. the necessary and proper clause
    C. the republican government clause
    D. the supremacy clause

    D (p. 84)

11. Which of the following, concerning federalism around the globe, is correct?
    A. By the 1990s, federalism was the most common structure of government.
    B. The United States, Canada, and Germany are the only federal systems in the world.
    C. Federalism remains a rare structure of government among the over 150 nations of the world.
    D. Federalism is found only in North America and Europe.

    C (p. 86)

12. What countries are most likely to have a governmental design based on federalism?
    A. countries consisting of one small ethnic, racial, or religious community
    B. countries containing different cultures, each located in a separate geographic area
    C. countries that have their roots in absolute monarchies
    D. countries wishing to promote agriculture and other aspects of a rural economy

    B (p. 86)

13. Why was the decision by Vermont to recognize gay and lesbian civil unions such a controversial issue of federalism?
    A. because the law was found to be in violation of the Fifth Amendment
    B. because the Constitution requires all states to honor and recognize the official acts of other states
    C. because the act was an attempt to enforce the restrictions against federal *habeas corpus* violations
    D. because Vermont did not get the approval of at least half the other states before passing the law

    B (p. 87)

14. The _____ clause of the Constitution requires that states normally recognize the laws, acts, and judicial decisions of other states.
    A. supremacy
    B. full faith and credit
    C. concurrent power
    D. double jeopardy

    B (p. 85)

15. What is the main purpose behind the privileges and immunities clause of Article IV?
    A. It prevents a state from giving special favors to its own residents or discriminating against nonresidents.
    B. It compels each state to recognize the laws of other states.
    C. It requires all states to provide a uniform standard of benefits and entitlement.
    D. It states that the Bill of Rights apply to the actions of state governments, as well as the national government.

    A (p. 87)

16. If a state grants a city the ability to govern its own local affairs, this delegation of power is known as
    A. home rule.
    B. dual federalism.
    C. ostracism.
    D. separation of powers.

    A (p. 88)

17. When the State of Alaska passed a law in the 1970s, giving state residents preference over nonresidents in obtaining work on oil pipelines, this law violated
    A. the interstate commerce clause.
    B. the full faith and credit clause.

C. the privileges and immunities clause.
D. the takings clause.

C (p. 87)

18. Which level of government is not mentioned at all in the federal Constitution?
    A. international affairs
    B. federal government
    C. state government
    D. city government

    D (p. 88)

19. Which of the following describes the constitutionally permitted relationship between the states?
    A. No state may ever enter into a contract or agreement with another state.
    B. No state shall enter into a contract or agreement with another state without the approval of Congress.
    C. States may have treaties with other states or with Indian reservations with the approval of Congress.
    D. The Senate controls all interstate relationships.

    B (p. 87)

20. According to the textbook, when was the era of dual federalism?
    A. from the ratification of the Constitution until the end of the Civil War
    B. from the ratification of the Constitution until the New Deal
    C. from the Civil War until World War II
    D. from the New Deal until the 1960s

    B (p. 89)

21. Which of the following was NOT a function of government most commonly performed by state governments during the era of dual federalism?
    A. commercial laws
    B. education
    C. patents and copyrights
    D. insurance laws

    C (p. 90)

22. During the era of dual federalism, what was the primary goal of the federal government's domestic policies?
   A. to promote competition between the states
   B. to assist the development of commercial activity within and between the states
   C. to protect citizens from the abuses of state governments
   D. to keep the states from going to war with each other

   B (p. 90)

23. Which level of government writes the majority of all criminal laws?
   A. the national government
   B. state governments
   C. local governments
   D. special districts

   B (p. 90)

24. How has the structure of federalism allowed for the longevity of the U.S. government?
   A. It has allowed for many divisive policy decisions to be made by states, rather than the national government.
   B. It has kept the national government rather small and aloof for most of American history.
   C. It has allowed states to develop in numerous and different ways.
   D. All of the above.

   D (pp. 90–91)

25. Which clause of the Constitution has been critical in allowing for the growth of national power?
   A. the commerce clause.
   B. the full faith and credit clause.
   C. the comity clause.
   D. the Tenth Amendment.

   A (p. 91)

26. What was the overall importance of the Supreme Court case *McCulloch v. Maryland*?
   A. The Supreme Court interpreted the delegated powers of Congress broadly, creating the potential for increased national powers.
   B. The Court gave a very restricted definition of Congress's delegated powers, in keeping with the era of dual federalism.
   C. The Court announced that dual federalism did not conform to the framer's design.
   D. The Supreme Court declared that all national banks were unconstitutional.

   A (p. 91)

27. What economic policy was the national government not allowed to perform during the nineteenth century?
    A. establish a series of national banks
    B. give patents and copyright protections
    C. regulate the health and safety of the workplace
    D. promote transportation between the states

    C (p. 92)

28. The constitutional idea of states' rights was strongest during which historical period?
    A. the years right before the Civil War
    B. reconstruction
    C. the Great Depression
    D. the 1960s

    A (p. 94)

29. Why was the Supreme Court case *United States v. Lopez* important?
    A. It was the first time since the New Deal that the Supreme Court limited the power of Congress found under the commerce clause.
    B. It was the first time that the Court had ever used the Tenth Amendment to limit the power of Congress.
    C. The Court found that citizens could not bring racial discrimination suits against state governments.
    D. The Court found the line-item veto unconstitutional.

    A (p. 96)

30. Which of the following statements best describes the trend in the Supreme Court's interpretation of federalism since the mid-1990s?
    A. The Court has slowly granted the national government more power over the states.
    B. The Court has limited the power of the national government over state governments.
    C. The Court has repeatedly declined to hear federalism cases, arguing that they are a political question.
    D. The Court has granted the states more access to sue the national government in federal courts.

    B (p. 96)

31. _____ describes the policy of delegating a policy program down to a lower level of government.
    A. Home rule
    B. Redistribution
    C. Devolution
    D. Preemption

    C (p. 95)

32. Which event did the most to cause the rise of a more active national government?
    A. the Civil War
    B. World War I
    C. the Great Depression
    D. the cold war

    C (p. 97)

33. When the national government appropriates money to the states, on the condition that it be spent as dictated by the national government, this money is called
    A. a grant-in-aid.
    B. an unfunded mandate.
    C. interstate commerce.
    D. devolution.

    A (p. 97)

34. What was an important reason for the declining importance of state governments during the 1960s?
    A. State governments were not raising enough revenue.
    B. The national government distrusted states due to the racism in the South.
    C. The national government was limited by the principle of home rule.
    D. State governments had delegated their powers to the national government.

    B (p. 99)

35. When the national government funds a project that is actually implemented by the states, this is an example of
    A. dual federalism.
    B. national supremacy.
    C. cooperative federalism.
    D. home rule.

    C (p. 99)

36. The term "marble cake" federalism is meant to refer to what development?
    A. Budgeting is conducted with a "dessert first" mentality.
    B. Intergovernmental cooperation has blurred the lines between different layers of government.
    C. The federal government bribes the states with various gifts in order to convince the states to follow national standards.
    D. After a few days, federalism becomes hard and tasteless.

    B (p. 99)

37. When the federal government sets environmental standards that every state must follow, this is an example of
    A. cooperative federalism.
    B. dual federalism.
    C. regulated federalism.
    D. marble cake federalism.

    C (p. 100)

38. The principle of _____ allows the federal government the power to override any state or local law in one particular area of policy.
    A. cooperative federalism
    B. grant-in-aid
    C. preemption
    D. dual federalism

    C (p. 100)

39. If the federal government compelled state governments to obey costly regulations but did not reimburse the costs, this is called a _____
    A. grant-in-aid.
    B. preemption.
    C. unfunded mandate.
    D. block grant.

    C (p. 101)

40. Disapproval over unfunded mandates is most common among those who want
    A. to reduce the power of the federal government.
    B. to increase the scope of federal regulations.
    C. to exercise a strong principle of preemption.
    D. a return to the days of national supremacy.

    A (p. 101)

41. Federal officials seeking to give state governments more authority are most likely to support
    A. unfunded mandates.
    B. preemption.
    C. block grants.
    D. categorical grants.

    C (p. 102)

42. The form of federal assistance called _____ provides money to state governments with no strings attached.
    A. New Federalism
    B. general revenue sharing
    C. block grants
    D. unfunded mandates

    B (p. 102)

43. What is one of the biggest problems with federal block grants?
    A. There is a need for greater accountability in how the funds are actually spent by the states
    B. There is a need to be sure that the states are following the precise regulations established by the federal government.
    C. There is a need to make sure they do not violate the commerce clause of the Constitution.
    D. Republican administrations have been unwilling to allow block grants.

    A (p. 103)

44. Welfare is the best-known type of _____ policy.
    A. regulatory
    B. distributive
    C. redistributive
    D. commercial

    C (p. 104)

45. During the 1990s, the number of persons on welfare
    A. increased sharply.
    B. declined slightly.
    C. declined dramatically.
    D. remained steady, despite reforms.

    C (p. 104)

46. Which president was behind the enactment of Social Security?
    A. Theodore Roosevelt
    B. Franklin D. Roosevelt
    C. John F. Kennedy
    D. Lyndon B. Johnson

    B (p. 105)

47. The primary welfare programs, such as food stamps, rent subsidies, and AFDC, made up _____ percent of the 1995 national budget.
    A. 5
    B. 15
    C. 25
    D. 35

    A (p. 105)

48. Many of the debates concerning federalism reflect
    A. the regional competition that has existed throughout American history.
    B. the greatest source of tension between Republicans and Democrats.
    C. differing views about the ultimate goal of government itself.
    D. conflict of interest problems between government officials and business leaders.

    C (p. 110)

49. Beyond voting, most forms of political participation take place at what level of government?
    A. national
    B. state and local
    C. international
    D. nonprofit

    B (p. 112)

50. The confusion amongst different government officials after the events of 9/11 demonstrates what about federalism in the United States?
    A. There has been a lack of coordination and communication among the various levels of government.
    B. Devolution of governmental power has been a danger to national security.
    C. Each state needs its own homeland security official.
    D. The police powers of the state governments need to be devolved to city and local officials.

    A (p. 111)

51. *Gibbons v. Ogden* (1824) was important because it
    A. fully developed the concept of judicial review.
    B. fully developed the concept of dual citizenship.
    C. established the supremacy of the national government in all matters affecting interstate commerce.
    D. determined that the forced relocation of the Five Civilized Tribes to Oklahoma was unconstitutional.

    C (pp. 91–92)

52. Block grants are designed to
    A. fund a large number of similar projects.
    B. fund urban improvements on a specific city block.
    C. give the states considerable say in how the money should be spent.
    D. fund capital improvements in a specific block of schools.

    C (p. 102)

53. One argument for a strong federal government is its role in ensuring _____ across states.
    A. liberty
    B. equality
    C. welfare reform
    D. laissez-faire capitalism

    B (p. 110)

TRUE OR FALSE

1. Federal systems are most commonly found in countries that have a highly homogeneous population.

    F (p. 84)

2. The Tenth Amendment gives the national government expressed powers over state governments.

    F (p. 84)

3. The full faith and credit clause demands that the U.S. government run a balanced budget.

    F (p. 85)

4. Local governments are not mentioned anywhere in the U.S. Constitution.

    T (p. 88)

5. Dual federalism describes the relationship between the national government and the states throughout the nineteenth century.

    T (p. 89)

6. *McCulloch v. Maryland* gave Congress potentially expansive powers for regulating commercial activity.

    T (p. 91)

7. Since the New Deal, the Supreme Court has never restricted Congress's power under the commerce clause.

    F (p. 96)

8. An unfunded mandate refers to the national government imposing regulatory costs on the states without reimbursement.

    T (p. 101)

9. In the 1990s, welfare policy was centralized by the national government.

    F (p. 104)

10. Federalism has allowed American democracy to be more flexible and diverse.

    T (p. 113)

CHAPTER 4 | Civil Liberties

MULTIPLE CHOICE

1. The Bill of Rights is
   A. the first ten amendments to the Constitution.
   B. all of the civil liberties and civil rights found in the Constitution.
   C. the first national Constitution in the United States.
   D. the First Amendment.

   A (p. 119)

2. The first ten amendments to the U.S. Constitution are called
   A. Magna Carta.
   B. the Articles of Confederation.
   C. the Mayflower Compact.
   D. the Bill of Rights.

   D (p. 119)

3. Which if the following is NOT a liberty protected by the Bill of Rights?
   A. the free exercise of religion
   B. freedom from unreasonable searches and seizures
   C. guarantee of the due process of law
   D. equal protection of the laws

   D (p. 119)

4. What was the main reason why Alexander Hamilton did not want a Bill of Rights?
   A. He wanted the government to have as much power as possible.
   B. He believed that too many individual liberties destroyed the trust between citizen and government.
   C. He believed it was unnecessary for a government that possessed only specifically delegated powers.
   D. A bill of rights, Hamilton believed, would make the Constitution too long and cumbersome.

   C (p. 121)

5. The Bill of Rights was written because
   A. anti-Federalists demanded one as the price of ratification of the Constitution.
   B. the Federalists realized that no constitution would last for long without a Bill of Rights.
   C. the federal government in the early days of the republic was violating too many individual rights.
   D. George Washington advocated the measure very forcefully.

   A (p. 122)

6. Which of the following is the best example of a substantive civil liberty?
   A. "The accused shall enjoy a right to a speedy trial."
   B. "Cruel and unusual punishments shall not be inflicted."
   C. "Congress shall make no law respecting the establishment of religion."
   D. "Private property shall not be taken for public use without just compensation."

   C (p. 119)

7. The due process clause of the Fifth Amendment is best described as
   A. a substantive civil liberty.
   B. a procedural civil liberty.
   C. a civil right.
   D. a delegated power.

   B (p. 119)

8. According to the textbook, what is the constitutional problem relating to the nationalization of the Bill of Rights?
   A. Does the Bill of Rights put limits only on the national government, or does it limit state governments as well?
   B. Does every state have to ratify each amendment to the Constitution, or only a majority of the states?

C. Must the level of enforcement of the Bill of Rights have to be equal throughout every state?
D. Does the Bill of Rights legalize a national moral consensus?

A (p. 122)

9. Which of the following is the best description of the Supreme Court's first ruling on the issue of the nationalization of the Bill of Rights in 1833?
   A. The takings clause restricts national and state government but not city governments.
   B. The Bill of Rights should not be used if the state's constitution already contains its own bill of rights.
   C. The takings clause does not cover accidents caused by government officials.
   D. The Bill of Rights limits only the national government but not state governments.

   D (p. 122)

10. The process by which the Supreme Court has expanded specific parts of the Bill of Rights to protect citizens against states as well as federal actions is called
    A. *habeas corpus.*
    B. selective incorporation.
    C. the takings clause.
    D. federalism.

    B (p. 124)

11. The wall of separation between church and state is best found in what clause of the Constitution?
    A. the free exercise clause
    B. the establishment clause
    C. the equal protection clause
    D. the wall of separation clause

    B (p. 126)

12. The Supreme Court has traditionally allowed government aid to religious schools only if the aid
    A. has a secular purpose.
    B. neither advances nor inhibits religion.
    C. does not excessively entangle government in the affairs of religious institutions.
    D. All of the above.

    D (p. 126)

13. The _____ of the First Amendment protects an individual's right to believe and practice whatever religion she or he chooses.
    A. establishment clause
    B. free association clause
    C. free exercise clause
    D. religious freedom restoration clause

    C (p. 127)

14. The Supreme Court case concerning smoking peyote during Native Americans' religious rituals demonstrates that the key problem for the Court in ruling on religious freedom is to determine
    A. the difference between religious beliefs and conduct that is based on religious beliefs.
    B. which religions are serious and which are not.
    C. which religious organizations are really illegal operations.
    D. who is a true believer or not.

    A (p. 127)

15. The Religious Freedom Restoration Act, passed by Congress in 1993, was an attempt to
    A. recognize Judeo-Christianity as the unofficial religion of the United States.
    B. give more protection to religious freedoms than the Supreme Court was allowing.
    C. establish a federal school voucher program.
    D. permit prayer in the public schools.

    B (p. 127)

16. Why was the Religious Freedom Restoration Act ruled unconstitutional by the Supreme Court?
    A. The Constitution forbids the establishment of official or unofficial religions.
    B. Peyote smoking is illegal, even if it is for religious reasons.
    C. The Court argued that only the judiciary can interpret the scope of the Bill of Rights.
    D. The president had not formally signed the act.

    C (p. 128)

17. What were the Alien and Sedition Acts?
    A. laws passed in the 1790s that made it a crime to say or publish anything that would defame the government of the United States
    B. laws that made it a crime for foreign immigrants to belong to the Communist Party or other anti-American organizations
    C. a law passed by Congress denying civil liberties to all noncitizens

D. laws passed during the Civil War denying Confederate sympathizers the right of free speech

A (p. 130)

18. The first time the Supreme Court interpreted the full scope of the First Amendment was
    A. in the 1790s, soon after the Bill of Rights was ratified.
    B. during the Civil War.
    C. in the years right after World War I.
    D. during the cold war.

    C (p. 130)

19. The first and most famous test for determining when the government could intervene to suppress political speech was called the
    A. speech plus test.
    B. clear and present danger test.
    C. strict scrutiny test.
    D. Lemon test.

    B (p. 130)

20. Which of the following would NOT be an example of speech plus?
    A. burning the American flag
    B. assassinating a political leader
    C. picketing a factory
    D. All are examples of speech plus.

    B (p. 132)

21. When the government blocks the publication of material it does not want released, this is known as
    A. sedition.
    B. speech plus.
    C. prior restraint.
    D. clear and present danger.

    C (p. 133)

22. The Supreme Court case of *Near v. Minnesota* established the principle that
    A. the government could block publication of newspapers during a time of crisis, like the cold war.
    B. only under the most extraordinary circumstances should the government prevent the publication of newspapers and magazines.
    C. news articles that were not truthful received no First Amendment protection.
    D. the news media could not publish obscene material.

    B (p. 133)

23. Which of the following forms of speech are given the highest level of protection by the Supreme Court?
    A. libel
    B. fighting words
    C. political sedition
    D. all of the above

    C (p. 133)

24. Which of the following types of speech does/do not receive full First Amendment protection?
    A. slander
    B. fighting words
    C. obscenity
    D. all of the above

    D (p. 133)

25. In order for a public official to win a libel suit against a news medium, the official must prove
    A. the story was false.
    B. the story was malicious.
    C. the story was false and malicious.
    D. Libelous stories receive absolute protection if the story is about a public official.

    C (pp. 133–34)

26. About what did Justice Potter Stewart confess "I know it when I see it"?
    A. fighting words
    B. speech inciting violence
    C. pornography
    D. sedition

    C (p. 134)

27. Which of the following statements regarding the law and the Internet is FALSE?
    A. The Internet has made it more difficult for government to regulate obscene material.
    B. The Internet receives more freedom from regulation than either radio or television.
    C. The Court has struck down several attempts by Congress to regulate the Internet.
    D. The Internet is subject to the same regulations as radio stations.

    D (p. 135)

28. The Court does not give full protection to fighting words because
    A. insults hurt people's feelings.
    B. such words are not part of the essential exposition of ideas.
    C. fighting words are a form of sedition.
    D. they are a form of obscenity.

    B (p. 135)

29. Which of the following is the most recent constitutional issue concerning fighting words?
    A. university harassment and hate speech codes
    B. racial profiling
    C. terrorist threats
    D. vulgar and offense satire and parodies

    A (p. 136)

30. Which of the following best reflects the Supreme Court's position on commercial speech, such as advertisements?
    A. Commercial speech receives no First Amendment protection.
    B. Advertisements receive limited First Amendment protection.
    C. Advertisements receive as much protection as anything else written in the newspaper.
    D. Commercial speech regulations depend on the commerce clause, not the Bill of Rights.

    B (p. 137)

31. Which of the following statements concerning the Second Amendment is FALSE?
    A. The Supreme Court has never nationalized the Second Amendment to cover state action.
    B. No gun control law has ever been held to violate the Second Amendment.
    C. The Court has ruled that the Second Amendment permits private citizen militias.
    D. The origin of the Second Amendment was based on the fact that state militias in the eighteenth century could not afford to supply firearms to militia members.

    C (pp. 138–39)

32. The Fourth, Fifth, Sixth and Eighth Amendments are largely about
    A. protections for those accused of committing a crime.
    B. the right to privacy and travel.
    C. the demand that citizens be treated equally.
    D. the limits of Congress regarding economic regulation.

    A (p. 140)

33. In criminal cases, the burden of proof lies on the
    A. government prosecutor.
    B. accused.
    C. victim.
    D. judge.

    A (p. 140)

34. The _____ rule forbids the introduction in trial of any piece of evidence obtained illegally.
    A. warrant
    B. exclusionary
    C. Miranda
    D. ex post facto

    B (p. 140)

35. What was the Supreme Court case that declared the exclusionary rule?
    A. *Miranda v. Arizona*
    B. *Near v. Minnesota*
    C. *Mapp v. Ohio*
    D. *Palko v. Connecticut*

    C (p. 140)

36. The Fourth Amendment protects against
    A. cruel and unusual punishments.
    B. unreasonable searches and seizures.
    C. self incrimination.
    D. quartering military troops in private homes.

    B (p. 140)

37. The controversy over suspicionless drug tests at school and in the workplace pits the government's war on drugs against the right
    A. against self-incrimination.
    B. against profiling.
    C. to take drugs.
    D. to privacy from unwarranted searches.

    D (p. 141)

38. What is a grand jury?
    A. the name for the juries used in the federal courts
    B. a jury that determines whether there is enough evidence to justify a trial
    C. the jury that determines the sentence, after guilt has been proven
    D. a jury that determines whether the accused's rights have been violated

    B (p. 142)

39. The right against _____ prevents persons from being tried twice for the same crime.
    A. self-incrimination
    B. double jeopardy
    C. exclusion
    D. unreasonable seizures

    B (p. 143)

40. Which of the following provisions of the Bill of Rights has NOT been nationalized?
    A. the right to a grand jury
    B. the right against double jeopardy
    C. the right to a lawyer
    D. All civil liberties have been nationalized.

    A (p. 142)

41. The requirement that persons under arrest be informed of their right to remain silent is known as the _____ rule.
    A. Mapp
    B. Gideon
    C. Miranda
    D. Palko

    C (p. 144)

42. The term "eminent domain" describes
    A. the power of the government to take private property for public use.
    B. the right of individuals not to have their property taken by the government.
    C. the power of the Supreme Court to declare the meaning and scope of all civil liberties.
    D. the power of the federal government to seize land owned and managed by states, in the public interest.

    A (p. 144)

43. The takings clause states that the government may not take private property
    A. for public use.
    B. without prior notification.
    C. without due compensation.
    D. without giving it back in due time.

    C (p. 144)

44. The case of *Gideon v. Wainwright* established the right
    A. to counsel in felony cases.
    B. against self-incrimination.
    C. to be warned of your rights at the time of arrest.
    D. against suspicionless searches and seizures.

    A (p. 146)

45. The Eighth Amendment prohibits
    A. double jeopardy.
    B. cruel and unusual punishment.
    C. denial of a lawyer in felony trials.
    D. the violation of *habeas corpus*.

    B (p. 146)

46. The different criminal penalties for possessing powder cocaine versus crack reflect
    A. a racial and class inconsistency in sentencing.
    B. a violation of the Eight Amendment.
    C. the power of eminent domain.
    D. the effect of the exclusionary rule in sentencing decisions.

    A (p. 146)

47. The current prohibition on states to criminalize abortion is based on
    A. the right to the due process of law.
    B. equal protection against sexual discrimination.
    C. the right to privacy.
    D. the right against cruel and unusual punishment.

    C (p. 151)

48. The right to privacy was formally articulated by the Supreme Court in a case involving
    A. a law criminalizing abortion.
    B. access to birth control.
    C. the right to die.
    D. the right to grow drugs for personal use.

    B (p. 150)

49. Since 1973, the right to an abortion has been
    A. upheld and expanded.
    B. upheld but narrowed in scope.
    C. overturned.
    D. The Supreme Court has not heard another case involving abortion since 1973.

    B (p. 151)

50. The USA PATRIOT Act, passed in the wake of 9/11, allows for
    A. warrantless searches of homes and offices.
    B. monitoring of Internet and e-mail activities.
    C. holding immigrants without charge if they are deemed a threat to national security.
    D. All of the above.

    D (p. 145)

51. The substantive constraints found in the Bill of Rights
    A. put limits on what government shall and shall not have the power to do.
    B. define how the government is supposed to act.
    C. define when the government is supposed to act.
    D. discuss why the government is or is not supposed to do something.

    A (p. 119)

52. The procedural restraints found in the Bill of Rights
    A. put limits on what government shall and shall not have the power to do.
    B. define how the government is supposed to act.
    C. define when the government is supposed to act.
    D. discuss why the government is or is not supposed to do something.

    B (p. 119)

53. The constitutional basis for the nationalization of the Bill of Rights is
    A. the First Amendment.
    B. the Fourteenth Amendment.
    C. *Plessy v. Ferguson.*
    D. *Roe v. Wade.*

    B (p. 123)

54. *Palko v. Connecticut* (1937) was significant because it established the principle of
    A. judicial review.
    B. judicial activism.
    C. comprehensive incorporation.
    D. selective incorporation.

    D (p. 124)

55. The establishment clause of the First Amendment has been interpreted as meaning that
    A. Congress has the power to establish a national church in the United States.
    B. Congress has the power to establish a national newspaper in the United States.
    C. a virtual wall of separation exists between church and state in the United States.
    D. civil liberties are well established and never subject to change in the United States.

    C (p. 126)

56. The *Lemon* test is a set of criteria developed to guide the Supreme Court in cases dealing with the issue of
    A. pornography.
    B. abortion.
    C. freedom of expression.
    D. separation of church and state.

    D (p. 126)

57. The free exercise clause of the First Amendment protects the right to
    A. own and use firearms.
    B. believe and to practice whatever religion one chooses.
    C. vote free from governmental interference.
    D. speak in public.

    B (p. 127)

58. The rights to assembly and petition are guaranteed by the same amendment guaranteeing
    A. free speech.
    B. due process.
    C. privacy.
    D. None of the above.

    A (p. 132)

59. The Second Amendment to the U.S. Constitution deals with
    A. the right to bear arms.
    B. the quartering of troops.
    C. due process.
    D. cruel and unusual punishment.

    A (p. 138)

60. "Due process of law" in the United States is generally defined by the
    A. First, Second, Third, and Fourth amendments.
    B. Second, Third, Fourth, and Fifth amendments.
    C. Fourth, Fifth, Sixth, and Eighth amendments.
    D. Seventh, Eighth, Ninth, and Tenth amendments.

    C (p. 140)

61. *Miranda* (1966) was important because it produced the rules that must be used
    A. to determine if separation between church and state has been violated.
    B. to judge whether printed materials are pornographic or not.
    C. to determine if some element of the Bill of Rights should be applied to the states.
    D. by the police before questioning an arrested criminal suspect.

    D (p. 144)

62. The Supreme Court case that established the right to counsel was
    A. *Miranda v. Arizona* (1966).
    B. *Roe v. Wade* (1973).
    C. *U.S. v. Nixon* (1973).
    D. *Gideon v. Wainwright* (1963).

    D (p. 146)

63. Protections against double jeopardy can be found in the
    A. Fourth Amendment.
    B. Fifth Amendment.
    C. Sixth Amendment.
    D. Seventh Amendment.

    B (p. 143)

64. The right to legal counsel in a criminal proceeding is guaranteed by the
    A. Fourth Amendment.
    B. Fifth Amendment.
    C. Sixth Amendment.
    D. Seventh Amendment.

    C (p. 146)

65. *Griswold v. Connecticut* (1965) and *Roe v. Wade* (1973) have been extremely important in the development of
    A. a constitutional right to privacy.
    B. American due process.
    C. New Federalism.
    D. a test which can be used to determine what is unprotected speech.

    A (pp. 150–51)

66. A woman's constitutional right to an abortion was established in
    A. *Gideon v. Wainwright* (1963).
    B. *Griswold v. Connecticut* (1965).
    C. *Miranda v. Arizona* (1966).
    D. *Roe v. Wade* (1973).

    D (p. 151)

67. Which of the following does NOT fall under constitutional arguments in favor of the right to privacy?
    A. right to abortion
    B. rights of homosexuals
    C. right to use pornography
    D. right to die

    C (pp. 150–52)

68. A recent controversy that has tested the constitutional definition of "search and seizure" has been
    A. prohibition against voluntary suicides.
    B. mandatory drug testing.
    C. employers reading employees' e-mail messages.
    D. mandatory waiting period for purchasing firearms.

    B (p. 141)

TRUE OR FALSE

1. The Bill of Rights actually contains civil liberties, not rights.

   T (p. 119)

2. The Supreme Court has ruled that every provision in the Bill of Rights protects the individual from actions by the states as well as the federal government.

   F (p. 124)

3. The free exercise clause establishes a wall of separation between church and state.

   F (p. 126)

4. School vouchers have recently become a controversy involving the relationship between church and state.

   T (p. 127)

5. The Constitution protects all political speech that is not an incitement to imminent lawless violence.

   T (p. 132)

6. It is unconstitutional to burn the American flag.

   F (p. 132)

7. Since the 1960s, slander and libel receive full First Amendment protection.

   F (p. 134)

8. The Supreme Court has ruled that the death penalty is a violation of the Eighth Amendment.

   F (p. 146)

9. The famous Miranda rule was recently overturned by the Supreme Court.

   F (p. 144)

10. The Supreme Court has ruled the Constitution protects the privacy right to engage in homosexual conduct.

    F (p. 152)

CHAPTER 5 | Civil Rights

MULTIPLE CHOICE

1. Which of the following is the key question behind civil rights protection?
   A. What are the limits to the government's powers over the individual?
   B. What is the proper meaning of equality?
   C. What is the appropriate role of the federal government?
   D. How has the expansion of the bureaucracy effected democracy?

   B (p. 161)

2. Which of the following best describes how to distinguish civil rights from civil liberties?
   A. Unlike civil liberties, civil rights place positive obligations on the government to take action.
   B. Unlike civil liberties, civil rights restrict and limit government action.
   C. Unlike civil liberties, only state governments enforce civil rights.
   D. Unlike civil liberties, civil rights protect corporations as well as individuals.

   A (p. 162)

3. When did civil rights become part of the U.S. Constitution?
   A. Civil rights have always been part of the Constitution.
   B. Civil rights were included in the Bill of Rights.
   C. Civil rights were incorporated with the ratification of the Fourteenth Amendment.
   D. Civil rights were incorporated when Congress passed the Civil Rights Act of 1964.

   C (p. 162)

4. How did women exercise political influence in the days before they could legally vote?
   A. Women often formed political parties, clubs, and associations that were often as politically effective as those formed by men.
   B. Women used their power as guardians of the moral realm to push for reform.
   C. While women could not vote, they were often elected to political offices.
   D. Women exercised little to no political influence before achieving the right to vote.

   B (p. 164)

5. What was the goal pursued by members of the abolitionist movement?
   A. the end of slavery
   B. the overthrow of the U.S. Constitution
   C. the removal of all tariffs on slave-produced goods
   D. the removal of all nonwhites from U.S. territory

   A (p. 163)

6. Which of the following persons is most associated with the abolitionist movement?
   A. James Madison
   B. William Lloyd Garrison
   C. Jefferson Davis
   D. Andrew Jackson

   B (p. 163)

7. What was the Seneca Falls Convention?
   A. a meeting in upstate New York in the mid–nineteenth century regarding women's rights
   B. an important gathering which initiated the abolitionist movement
   C. a convention of southern leaders in the 1850s debating succession
   D. the convention that wrote and debated the Fourteenth Amendment

   A (p. 164)

8. Which of the following statements about the Reconstruction era is FALSE?
   A. African Americans held many political offices in the South.
   B. Many parts of the southern states were occupied by federal troops.
   C. The Constitution was amended three times.
   D. African American voters supported the Democratic Party.

   D (p. 165)

9. The Civil Rights Act of 1875 attempted to
   A. protect African Americans from discrimination in public accommodations like hotels and theaters.
   B. protect African Americans against disenfranchisement in the voting booth.
   C. expand the protections of the Fourteenth Amendment to recent Asian immigrants.
   D. restore the lost civil rights for former Confederate soldiers and sympathizers.

   A (p. 165)

10. What was the Supreme Court's response to the Civil Rights Act of 1875?
    A. It declared the act constitutional.
    B. It declared the act unconstitutional because it protected against acts of private discrimination, not state discrimination.
    C. It declared the act unconstitutional because Congress had violated the principles of federalism.
    D. The Supreme Court never heard a case concerning the constitutionality of this act.

    B (p. 165)

11. During the late nineteenth century, the equal protection clause was
    A. used as a strong tool for engineering racial equality.
    B. severely limited in scope by the Supreme Court.
    C. ruled to be unconstitutional.
    D. more strongly defended by individual states than by the federal government.

    B (pp. 165–66)

12. Which of the following practices was explicitly protected by the "separate but equal" principle?
    A. segregated schools
    B. white primaries
    C. poll taxes
    D. restrictive covenants

    A (p. 166)

13. To what does the term "Jim Crow" refer?
    A. It refers to northern whites who sympathized with African Americans.
    B. It refers to the civil rights movement of the mid–twentieth century.
    C. It refers to the system of racial segregation in the South after Reconstruction.
    D. It refers to African American politicians during Reconstruction.

    C (p. 165)

14. The Supreme Court's ruling in *Plessy v. Ferguson*
    A. announced the separate but equal rule.
    B. upheld the Civil Rights Act of 1875.
    C. declared that segregation by race was unconstitutional.
    D. ruled the equal protection clause did not cover private acts of discrimination.

    A (p. 166)

15. After World War II, what was the first government institution to begin drawing attention to the problem of racism in American life?
    A. the Supreme Court
    B. the White House
    C. Congress
    D. State governments

    B (p. 167)

16. The NAACP had the most success with which of the following political strategies for combating racism?
    A. mass marches and protests
    B. civil disobedience
    C. lawsuits
    D. passive resistance

    C (p. 168)

17. During the late 1940s and 1950s, _____ was the head lawyer for the NAACP Legal Defense Fund.
    A. John Marshall
    B. Thurgood Marshall
    C. James Byrnes
    D. Fredrick Douglass

    B (p. 168)

18. What was the Supreme Court's record in segregation cases in the years before *Brown v. Board of Education*?
    A. The Court overturned forms of segregation, using the separate but equal rule on factual grounds.
    B. The Court had struck down forms of segregation, but by using the commerce clause, not the Fourteenth Amendment.
    C. The Court had already struck down separate but equal as a principle before *Brown*.
    D. There had been no major challenges to segregation before *Brown*.

    A (p. 168)

19. "Strict scrutiny" is the level of judicial review the federal courts give to all cases that involve
    A. racial classifications.
    B. gender classifications.
    C. age classifications.
    D. All of the above.

    A (p. 169)

20. Which of the following best summarizes the Supreme Court's ruling in *Brown v. Board of Education*?
    A. Racially segregated schools can never be equal.
    B. States that segregate need to spend more money to make African American schools equal.
    C. The federal judiciary, but not Congress, has the power to enforce civil rights.
    D. School segregation was unfair but did not violate the Fourteenth Amendment.

    A (p. 169)

21. In their response to *Brown v. Board of Education*, southern states did all of the following EXCEPT
    A. pass laws requiring schools to remain segregated.
    B. centralize school boards, to prevent local districts from obeying the Supreme Court.
    C. protest the constitutionality of the Court's decision.
    D. quickly desegregate the schools.

    D (p. 169)

22. Which of the following areas of discrimination was/were not touched by the legal principles of *Brown v. Board of Education*?
    A. voting
    B. racially discriminatory jury selection
    C. public accommodations
    D. all of the above

    D (p. 169)

23. Legally enforced segregation in public schools is a form of _____ discrimination.
    A. de facto
    B. de jure
    C. stare decisis
    D. ex post facto

    B (p. 169)

24. What is the name for the type of school segregation that is the result of racially divided neighborhoods, rather than state laws?
    A. de facto
    B. de jure
    C. stare decisis
    D. ex post facto

    A (p. 169)

25. Why did President Dwight Eisenhower deploy federal troops to Little Rock, Arkansas, in 1957?
    A. because there were massive race riots as a result of the order to desegregate the schools
    B. because the governor of Arkansas had brought in the state's National Guard to help resist desegregation
    C. because the Ku Klux Klan were making terrorist threats against state officials if the local school district tried to integrate
    D. because there was the fear that communists had infiltrated the local government

    B (p. 171)

26. What forbade discrimination based on race in the workplace?
    A. the Fourteenth Amendment
    B. the Civil Rights Act of 1875
    C. the Civil Rights Act of 1964
    D. the Nineteenth Amendment

    C (p. 177)

27. The Civil Rights Act of 1964 was
    A. the first civil rights law Congress had ever passed.
    B. the first civil rights law Congress has passed since Reconstruction.
    C. the third civil rights bill passed by Congress since *Brown v. Board of Education.*
    D. the last civil rights bill passed by Congress.

    C (p. 173)

28. Which of the following areas was NOT covered by the Civil Rights Act of 1964?
    A. employment
    B. public accommodations
    C. school desegregation
    D. poll taxes

    D (p. 175)

58 | Chapter 5

29. Which city was the setting for a major racial confrontation concerning school busing?
   A. Atlanta
   B. Boston
   C. Dallas
   D. Miami

   B (pp. 176–77)

30. Which of the following best describes the trend in the federal courts toward school desegregation since the 1990s?
   A. The courts have increased the federal supervision of local school desegregation.
   B. The courts have decreased the federal supervision of local school desegregation.
   C. Federal courts have continued the active use of busing.
   D. Federal courts have ordered the withdrawal of federal education funds for school districts that do not combat de facto desegregate.

   B (p. 177)

31. In a case of workplace discrimination, which government institution would most likely handle the complaint?
   A. the Supreme Court
   B. Congress
   C. the Equal Employment Opportunity Commission
   D. the Department of Commerce

   C (p. 178)

32. To draw voting districts so that one group or party is unfairly advantaged is called
   A. disenfranchisement.
   B. gerrymandering.
   C. busing.
   D. logrolling.

   B (p. 179)

33. Which of the following was NOT used as a way to prevent African Americans from voting?
   A. poll taxes
   B. literacy tests
   C. restrictive covenants
   D. white primaries

   C (p. 178)

34. To what does the term "redlining" refer?
    A. the practice of banks refusing to make loans to people living in certain neighborhoods
    B. the practice of drawing districts that are biased against minority groups
    C. denying one the right to vote by drawing a red line through a citizen's name in the voter registry
    D. the practice of denying someone rights by labeling him or her a communist

    A (p. 180)

35. The attempt to ratify the Equal Rights Amendment was an important political struggle for
    A. African Americans.
    B. Native Americans.
    C. women.
    D. gays and lesbians.

    C (p. 181)

36. At what level of scrutiny do courts review cases involving gender discrimination?
    A. strict scrutiny
    B. intermediate scrutiny
    C. rational basis
    D. none of the above

    B (p. 183)

37. A plaintiff may successfully bring a sexual harassment charge under what condition?
    A. only if the plaintiff can prove both economic and psychological harm
    B. only if the plaintiff can prove either economic or psychological harm
    C. The plaintiff need prove neither economic nor psychological harm.
    D. Only quid pro quo forms of harassment may be brought into court.

    C (p. 185)

38. Which of the following is NOT the name of a Latino civil rights organization?
    A. G.I. Forum
    B. LULAC
    C. NOW
    D. MALDEF

    C (p. 186)

39. Which group was excluded from immigrating to the United States from the late nineteenth century until the 1940s?
    A. Chinese
    B. Japanese
    C. Mexicans
    D. Russians

    A (p. 188)

40. *United States v. Wong Kim Ark* is an important case because it declared that
    A. the Exclusion Act was unconstitutional.
    B. anyone born in the United States was entitled to be a citizen.
    C. Asian American children could go to school with white students.
    D. English was not the official language of the United States.

    B (p. 188)

41. What was the purpose of California's Proposition 187?
    A. It barred illegal immigrants from voting.
    B. It barred illegal immigrants from receiving most public services.
    C. It barred illegal immigrants from ever receiving green cards.
    D. It attempted to limit illegal immigration at the border through the use of racial profiling.

    B (p. 188)

42. Before the 1920s, what was the political status of Native Americans?
    A. They were federal citizens but not citizens of the states in which they lived.
    B. They were considered as foreigners, because their tribes were regarded as separate nations.
    C. They were considered to be illegal immigrants, unless on reservations.
    D. They had no political status.

    B (p. 189)

43. The rights of the disabled not to be discriminated against in employment and access to public businesses is guaranteed by
    A. the Civil Rights Act of 1964.
    B. the Americans with Disabilities Act of 1990.
    C. the amended Civil Rights Act of 1991
    D. the federal courts, not by laws passed by Congress.

    B (p. 190)

44. What did the Supreme Court rule in *Bowers v. Hardwick*?
    A. There was a constitutional right to privacy for consensual homosexual activity.
    B. There was no constitutional right to privacy for consensual homosexual activity.

C. Civil rights protection was extended to gays and lesbians as a class.
D. The Court legalized gay marriages.

B (p. 191)

45. Who inaugurated government affirmative action programs?
    A. Franklin D. Roosevelt
    B. Dwight D. Eisenhower
    C. Lyndon B. Johnson
    D. Richard M. Nixon

    C (p. 192)

46. What Supreme Court case restricted the use of racial quotas in university admissions programs?
    A. *Brown v. Board of Education*
    B. *Board of Regents v. Bakke*
    C. *Bowers v. Hardwick*
    D. *Romer v. Evans*

    B (p. 194)

47. The Supreme Court case of *Adarand Constructors v. Pena* _____ affirmative action.
    A. strengthened
    B. weakened
    C. rendered unconstitutional
    D. ignored

    B (p. 194)

48. Which of the following best describes the *Hopwood* case?
    A. A federal court of appeals declared that race could never be used in public university admissions decisions.
    B. The Supreme Court overturned its *Bakke* decision.
    C. The Texas Supreme Court declared that racial quotas could be used in admission decisions to graduate schools and law schools.
    D. The U.S. Supreme Court stated that affirmative action violates the Fourteenth Amendment.

    A (p. 195)

49. What was President Bill Clinton's approach toward affirmative action policies?
    A. Clinton was a strong believer in the active use of affirmative action.
    B. Clinton wanted to reform but not end affirmative action programs.
    C. Clinton was a firm opponent to affirmative action.
    D. By the 1990s, there were no federal affirmative action programs for Clinton to oversee.

    B (p. 195)

50. To believe in the principle of _____ means that you believe that it is a violation of civil rights for the government ever to make decisions on the basis of race, even as a remedy for past discrimination.
    A. color blindness
    B. affirmative action
    C. equality of opportunity
    D. pro-choice

    A (p. 196)

51. Proposition 209, passed by California voters in 1996, did what?
    A. added civil rights protections for gays and lesbians to the state Constitution
    B. prohibited all use of affirmative action by state or local governments
    C. protected illegal aliens from discrimination by government agents
    D. allowed use of race for university admission policies but not for hiring or government contracts

    B (p. 196)

52. California's Proposition 209 and the *Hopwood* decision were met by
    A. widespread support in public opinion.
    B. controversy and political protests on both sides of the debate.
    C. public indifference.
    D. violence.

    B (p. 196)

53. Since September 11, which of the following has arisen as a civil rights concern?
    A. the use of racial profiling of persons who look Arabic
    B. the detention in prisons of persons of Arab descent who may not be charged with a crime
    C. the decline in a belief in the presumption of innocence
    D. All of the above.

    D (p. 187)

54. Approximately how many Americans of Japanese descent were sent to relocation camps during World War II?
    A. 2,700
    B. 53,000
    C. 120,000
    D. 1,400,000

    C (p. 187)

55. Most of the positive actions of government associated with the civil rights issue in the United States stem from application of
   A. the civil rights clause of Article VI of the U.S. Constitution.
   B. the commerce clause of Article I of the U.S. Constitution.
   C. the Tenth Amendment to the U.S. Constitution.
   D. the equal protection clause of the Fourteenth Amendment to the U.S. Constitution.

   D (p. 162)

56. Which amendments to the U.S. Constitution seemed to offer African Americans the most hope for achieving full citizenship rights in the United States?
   A. the First, Second, and Third
   B. the Fifth, Sixth, and Seventh
   C. the Thirteenth, Fourteenth, and Fifteenth
   D. the Twentieth, Twenty-First, and Twenty-Second

   C (p. 164)

57. The significance of the Nineteenth Amendment to the U.S. Constitution was that it
   A. created a national income tax.
   B. guaranteed women the right to vote.
   C. ended slavery.
   D. initiated prohibition.

   B (p. 167)

58. Women were guaranteed the right to vote with the passage of the Nineteenth Amendment, which was ratified in
   A. 1820.
   B. 1880.
   C. 1920.
   D. 1970.

   C (p. 167)

59. In the Civil Rights Act of 1964, Congress vastly expanded the role of the executive branch and the credibility of court orders by
   A. mandating that the southern states racially gerrymander their legislative districts to ensure that more African Americans were elected to Congress.
   B. creating the strict scrutiny test.
   C. creating a Department of Civil Rights.
   D. requiring that federal grants-in-aid to state and local governments for education be withheld from any school system practicing racial segregation.

   D (p. 175)

60. Desegregating schools in the northern states has proven very difficult because
    A. very few minorities live in the North.
    B. segregation in the North is generally *de facto*, the product of segregated housing and thousands of acts of private discrimination, which are hard to prove.
    C. discrimination in the South is so visible and pervasive that little attention is given to other parts of the country.
    D. there is less hostility to segregation in the North.

    B (p. 177)

61. One step taken toward the desegregation of public schools was
    A. busing children from poor urban school districts to wealthier suburban ones.
    B. the outlawing of all forms of *de facto* segregation.
    C. the opening of numerous private schools and academies.
    D. all of the above.

    A (p. 177)

62. The Twenty-Fourth Amendment to the U.S. Constitution strengthened voting rights by
    A. making poll taxes unconstitutional.
    B. making literacy tests unconstitutional.
    C. giving women the right to vote.
    D. giving Native Americans the right to vote.

    A (p. 178)

63. The right to vote was strengthened in 1975 when Congress
    A. made literacy tests mandatory for presidential elections.
    B. made literacy tests illegal and mandated bilingual ballots or other assistance for non-English-speaking Americans.
    C. gave women the right to vote.
    D. gave eighteen-year-olds the right to vote.

    B (p. 178)

64. An important consequence of Title VII of the 1964 Rights Act was that
    A. different segments of society were encouraged to convert goals and grievances into questions of rights.
    B. women were discouraged from participating in the political process.
    C. universal public education was made compulsory for all Americans.
    D. electoral participation in presidential elections was made mandatory for all Americans.

    A (p. 181)

65. The civil rights of Latinos and Asian Americans were assisted by the U.S. Supreme Court's ruling that
    A. school districts were required to provide bilingual education to non-English-speaking students.
    B. school districts must provide instruction that students can understand.
    C. bilingual ballots must be provided in several different languages.
    D. literacy tests were unconstitutional.

    B (p. 188)

66. A major civil rights concern to Latinos and Asian Americans is
    A. the extension of voting rights to include their groups.
    B. the abolishment of literacy tests.
    C. the treatment of legal and illegal immigrants.
    D. that they be granted full citizenship.

    C (p. 188)

67. The civil rights of Native Americans were strengthened by
    A. the Supreme Court's decision to allow Native Americans to be taught in their own language.
    B. winning federal recognition of their sovereignty, allowing the establishment of casino gambling on Indian lands.
    C. the success of the Native American Legal Defense Fund.
    D. both A and B.

    D (p. 189)

68. Affirmative action in the United States involves
    A. compensatory action to overcome the consequences of past discrimination.
    B. mandatory strict hiring quotas, established by the Department of Labor, for all federal agencies and programs.
    C. initiating lawsuits against the U.S. government for its past discriminatory practices.
    D. all of the above.

    A (p. 191)

69. Challenges to affirmative action have arisen not only in the Courts but also
    A. from President Bush.
    B. from the NAACP.
    C. through a national referendum.
    D. through state and local referendums.

    D (p. 196)

70. While all explicit _____ barriers to minorities have been eliminated in the United States, some _____ hindrances still exist.
    A. *de jure; de facto*
    B. *de facto; de jure*
    C. *habeas corpus; certiorari*
    D. theoretical; practical
    A (p. 201)

TRUE OR FALSE

1. The women's rights movement was often linked with the abolitionist movement during the nineteenth century.
    T (p. 163)

2. After *Brown v. Board of Education*, schools in the South quickly desegregated.
    F (p. 169)

3. If any law explicitly distinguishes by race, it is up to the government to prove that it does not violate the constitution.
    T (p. 169)

4. Under the Civil Rights Act, plaintiffs must show that an employer deliberately discriminated against them in order to win a lawsuit.
    F (p. 178)

5. The Voters Right Act of 1965 led to immediate gains in the number of African Americans registered to vote in the South.
    T (p. 179)

6. A federal commission found that in the 2000 election, African American precincts in Florida had three times the number of rejected ballots as white precincts.
    T (pp. 179–80)

7. Since the 1960s, the number of groups seeking protection of their civil rights has decreased.
    F (p. 181)

8. Courts have found sexual harassment on the job to be a form of sex discrimination.
    T (p. 184)

9. During World War II, over about 120,000 Americans of German descent were sent to relocation camps because of their ancestry.
    F (p. 187)

10. The events of September 11 and the war on terrorism have lead to new possible threats to civil liberties and civil rights.
    T (p. 187)

CHAPTER 6 | Public Opinion

MULTIPLE CHOICE

1. Civic education can best be defined as
   A. the necessary role of government to teach citizens ways in which they can help influence the government.
   B. the importance of government to teach citizens to be satisfied with their government.
   C. the law that requires students in public schools to pass a test showing a minimum level of knowledge in government.
   D. the manner in which the people educates government on what they want.

   A (p. 209)

2. What is the most common way students in school are educated about government?
   A. organizing protest marches
   B. learning legislative procedures by making laws
   C. holding student elections
   D. holdIng mock trials

   C (p. 209)

3. Attitudes that citizens hold about political issues, events, and people are called
   A. public opinions.
   B. political values.
   C. public ideologies.
   D. political propaganda.

   A (p. 211)

68 | Chapter 6

4. A political ideology is best defined as
   A. the specific preferences individuals have on an issue.
   B. the basic principles that shape particular attitudes.
   C. a cohesive set of beliefs that form a general philosophy about government.
   D. the concrete interests that people try to defend through public policy.

   C (p. 211)

5. Liberalism and conservatism are good examples of
   A. public opinions.
   B. political attitudes.
   C. political ideologies
   D. political interests.

   C (p. 211)

6. Which of the following describe the fundamental American political values?
   A. liberal and conservative
   B. Republican and Democrat
   C. internationalist and isolationist
   D. liberty, equality, and democracy

   D (p. 212)

7. Fundamental political values
   A. unify Americans in a common set of goals for government.
   B. divide Americans, who are in sharp disagreement over political values.
   C. are so vague as to be nearly useless in political debate.
   D. are not found in a nation as diverse as the United States.

   A (p. 212)

8. What percentage of Americans polled say they support free speech regardless of the views expressed?
   A. 45 percent
   B. 62 percent
   C. 75 percent
   D. 89 percent

   D (p. 212)

9. What reasons have scholars offered to explain why Americans are so united in terms of their overall goals for government?
   A. Unlike Europe, there was no feudal aristocracy in the United States.
   B. Unlike Europe, there has been no mainstream socialist movement in the United States.

C. Both A and B.
D. Neither A nor B.

C (p. 214)

10. The fact that affirmative action is so controversial reveals that
    A. Americans are divided over the importance of equal opportunity.
    B. different policy outcomes can be based on the same fundamental principle.
    C. Americans are forever separated by racial differences.
    D. Americans are very politically active.

    B (p. 214)

11. What values do supporters of legalized gay marriages use to support their position?
    A. Not to allow gay couples to marry is a violation of their equal rights.
    B. Gay marriages are an important form of affirmative action for gays and lesbians.
    C. Homophobia is a violation of the Constitution.
    D. Gay marriages save the government money.

    A (p. 215)

12. Which of the following are causes for differences in political opinions?
    A. race
    B. income
    C. education
    D. all of the above

    D (pp. 214, 218)

13. The process by which underlying political values are formed is known as
    A. political socialization.
    B. ideological education.
    C. brainwashing.
    D. value enhancing.

    A (p. 219)

14. A person's political party preference is primarily acquired through the influence of
    A. her or his family.
    B. the region of the country she or he lives in.
    C. her or his education.
    D. the media she or he consumes.

    A (p. 220)

15. Which of the following is NOT an important agency of socialization?
    A. family
    B. membership in social groups
    C. education
    D. All of the above are important agencies of socialization.

    D (p. 219)

16. Which of the following is the most likely cause for the differences between African and white Americans concerning the O. J. Simpson trial?
    A. The opinions of African and white Americans did not in fact differ much
    B. African and white Americans hold different political values.
    C. African and white Americans have different perspectives and experiences with the criminal justice system.
    D. African and white Americans have different levels of sports appreciation.

    C (p. 220)

17. What does the term "gender gap" refer to?
    A. the differences in voting behavior between men and women
    B. the differences in income and education levels in men and women
    C. differing levels of political participation between the genders
    D. the differences in fundamental political values held by men and women

    A (p. 221)

18. Which of the following phenomena CANNOT be explained by the gender gap?
    A. More women than men vote for Democrats.
    B. More women tend to favor government measures to protect the environment, compared with men.
    C. Men are more likely to join labor unions and other social organizations.
    D. Men are more likely to be more militaristic on issues of war and peace, compared with women.

    C (p. 221)

19. Why are groups and associations so critical to the formation of political opinions?
    A. Individuals often consciously or unconsciously adopt the views of groups with which they identify.
    B. Individuals are unable to come to opinions without the support of others to agree with them.
    C. Groups and associations are essential for publicizing the opinion of individuals.

D. Groups provide a way to change the opinions derived from the individual's family.

A (p. 223)

20. What did James Madison identify as the greatest source of political conflict for the United States?
    A. racial inequalities
    B. geographic differences
    C. the differences between the rich and the poor
    D. the conflicts between central government and local government

    C (p. 223)

21. What is the key difference between those who have gone to college and those who have not?
    A. Those with college education are usually more liberal.
    B. Those who have gone to college are typically more conservative than those who have not.
    C. There is a higher level of political participation among those with college education.
    D. College graduates are less likely to hold mainstream American values, than people without higher education.

    C (p. 224)

22. The movement of many white southerners from the Democratic to the Republican Party is a good example of
    A. the shifting political values of white southerners over time.
    B. the changes in political conditions and circumstances in the South, rather than in opinions or values.
    C. the growing conservative ideology in the South.
    D. the rise of labor unions and other associations in the South.

    B (p. 225)

23. A liberal would most likely support
    A. an expansion in government social services.
    B. an increase in the federal military budget.
    C. prayer in public schools.
    D. All of the above.

    A (pp. 226–27)

24. Opposition to legalized abortion is a position most likely supported by
    A. liberals.
    B. conservatives.
    C. libertarians.
    D. B and C.

    B (p. 227)

Chapter 6

25. In a liberal ideology, which of the core American values is the most important?
    A. liberty
    B. democracy
    C. equality
    D. justice

    C (p. 227)

26. _____ is the core political value prized most highly by American conservatives.
    A. democracy
    B. liberty
    C. equality
    D. family

    B (p. 227)

27. Conservatives are more likely than liberals to support
    A. the military.
    B. the status quo.
    C. the traditional family.
    D. All of the above.

    D (p. 227)

28. Political ideologies can best be understood as
    A. clear and logically consistent doctrines.
    B. open and fluid sets of general characteristics.
    C. relatively new elements of American political culture.
    D. established by the U.S. Constitution.

    B (p. 228)

29. People's underlying beliefs and ideologies
    A. compel them to think carefully about each opinion that they hold.
    B. color their perceptions so that they often may make automatic judgments on particular issues.
    C. prevent liberals and conservatives from sharing similar core values.
    D. are established when people are young and rarely change as they get older.

    B (p. 229)

30. Studies of political opinion show that
    A. most people do not hold specific and clearly defined opinions on all political issues.
    B. people's ideologies guide them in coming to an opinion on almost all political issues.

C. people understand what is in their interest, with or without political knowledge.
D. most Americans are keenly interested in how their government works.

A (p. 230)

31. The ability of citizens to influence government through a knowledge and interest in politics is called
    A. political saliency.
    B. core American values.
    C. political efficacy.
    D. the status quo effect.

    C (p. 231)

32. Recent studies by political scientists have shown
    A. Americans' knowledge of politics is generally high.
    B. the average American exhibits little knowledge of political institutions, processes, or leaders.
    C. there is actually little connection between possessing political knowledge and being an effective citizen.
    D. it is often difficult for the people seeking knowledge about government to actually find such information.

    B (p. 230)

33. The idea of a marketplace of ideas refers to
    A. important changes in copyright and patent laws that have restricted Americans' access to free information.
    B. the competition between competing opinions and ideas that is aired in the public forum.
    C. the use of opinion pollsters who will market a politician's speeches, ideas, and votes.
    D. the explosion of information brought on by the Internet and other advances in electronic communication.

    B (p. 231)

34. The marketplace of ideas has led to
    A. a sharp decline in knowledge among those too poor to purchase their information.
    B. a common ground on which Americans can debate and influence each others' opinions.
    C. a vulgar and often violent culture of argument, which may often require government regulation to keep the peace.
    D. the rise of large centralized multimedia corporations.

    B (p. 231)

74 | Chapter 6

35. Which of the following shapes public opinion?
    A. government
    B. private groups
    C. news media
    D. all of the above

    D (p. 231)

36. Which of the following best characterized the relationship between the Clinton White House and public opinion polls?
    A. Clinton relied heavily on public opinion polling to determine which positions to adopt.
    B. Positions taken by the Clinton White House were usually defined by the president's competition with Congress.
    C. Clinton used public opinion data sparingly, preferring to take his cues from the use of elite media organizations.
    D. The Clinton White House depended on advice from interest groups and the Democratic Party in order to build successful strategies.

    A (p. 232)

37. Political ideas
    A. most often erupt spontaneously from the American people.
    B. are usually produced and marketed to the public by various interest groups, think tanks, and political parties.
    C. are not allowed to return to the marketplace of ideas if they fail to be productive.
    D. are created by people who will receive a direct financial benefit from their adoption.

    B (p. 235)

38. Which of the following is NOT an organization committed to developing and marketing conservative ideas and policies?
    A. Heritage Foundation
    B. Hoover Institute
    C. Common Cause
    D. American Enterprise Institute

    C (p. 235)

39. Each of the following is a liberal organization EXCEPT
    A. the Sierra Club.
    B. the National Organization for Women.
    C. the Physicians for Social Responsibility.
    D. the chamber of commerce.

    D (p. 236)

40. Which of the following statements concerning the news media is NOT true?
   A. The ways in which the media reports news helps to shape the underlying attitudes and opinions of those consuming the news.
   B. In a free democracy, the news media provides information, without framing or interpreting it in any particular way.
   C. The news media is often a tool for politicians to use.
   D. The amount of investigative reporting has increased in the past thirty years.

   B (p. 236)

41. Which of the following about public opinion polls is NOT true?
   A. Polling is an attempt to make opinion gathering more scientific.
   B. Abraham Lincoln and Stephen Douglas were the first politicians to use public opinion polls.
   C. Polling is a way for politicians to experience public opinion in a large modern democracy.
   D. Politicians use polls in order to help them make decisions, as well as to gauge the reaction to decisions they have already made.

   B (p. 237)

42. The small group selected by pollsters to represent the entire population is called the
   A. validity quotient.
   B. sample.
   C. quota.
   D. hypothesis.

   B (p. 237)

43. The typical margin of error in a sample survey is
   A. 0.1 percent.
   B. 0.5 percent.
   C. 3 percent.
   D. 10 percent.

   C (p. 237)

44. Errors in polling, like poor question format, effect the polls'
   A. validity.
   B. bellwether effect.
   C. quota.
   D. hypothesis.

   A (p. 238)

76 | Chapter 6

45. When a politician who uses polling data believes an issue is more important to people than it actually is, she or he has fallen for the _____
    A. "bounce" effect.
    B. illusion of central tendency.
    C. illusion of saliency.
    D. bellwether effect.

    C (p. 241)

46. If I decide to support a candidate because I see that he or she is the front runner in a poll, I become an example of
    A. the bellwether effect.
    B. the illusion of saliency.
    C. the bandwagon effect.
    D. the poll pushing.

    C (p. 241)

47. The failure of major pollsters to predict Jesse Ventura's 1998 victory in Minnesota's gubernatorial election demonstrates that
    A. pollsters placed too much emphasis on the candidates of the two major parties.
    B. poll researchers polled only people who had voted before, ignoring potential new voters.
    C. poll takers believed that voters would actually show up to vote if they said they would.
    D. the wording of the polls overemphasized Ventura's past career in wrestling.

    B (pp. 242–43)

48. The practice of poll pushing involves
    A. the attempt of polling services like Harris or Gallop to sell major news media their polling data at a higher price during election seasons.
    B. the technique of calling people during dinner and in the evening, to assure that as many people as possible will be home.
    C. the technique of asking loaded questions in order to subtly shape the respondent's opinion.
    D. the effect that polls have to push politicians to adopt policy proposals they would not otherwise adopt.

    C (p. 240)

49. Which of the following is NOT a common opinion expressed by citizens of eastern and central Europe since the fall of communism?
    A. There is a general dissatisfaction with democracy.

B. There is growing disenchantment with market capitalism.
C. There is a desire for more aid and intervention from the United States and western Europe.
D. There is a concern for human rights violations.

C (p. 245)

50. School busing and military intervention in Bosnia and Haiti are two examples of
    A. how American policy responds quickly to negative public opinion.
    B. how American's opinions about an issue can be changed by politicians using polling data.
    C. how some government policies are implemented even without support from public opinion.
    D. how American policy is usually poll tested before it is implemented.

    C (p. 244)

51. What is an initiative?
    A. the set of questions asked in a public opinion survey
    B. a procedure that allows for laws to by placed on the ballot to be voted on by the electorate
    C. the policy proposals that stem directly from one's political ideologies
    D. a bill submitted to Congress before it becomes a law

    B (p. 244)

52. The term "public opinion" is used to describe
    A. the collected speeches and writings made by a president during his term in office.
    B. the analysis of events broadcast by news reporters during the evening news.
    C. the beliefs and attitudes that people have about issues.
    D. decisions of the U.S. Supreme Court.

    C (p. 211)

53. The complex set of beliefs and values that, as a whole, form a general philosophy about government is called
    A. public opinion.
    B. political ideology.
    C. political socialization.
    D. political efficacy.

    B (p. 211)

54. The difference between a political value and a political attitude is that
    A. values are conservative while attitudes are liberal.
    B. values are held for the short term while attitudes are held for the long term.
    C. values are basic principles while attitudes are specific preferences.
    D. there is no difference.

    C (p. 211)

55. While an individual's underlying beliefs help shape opinions on particular issues, two other important factors are
    A. a person's knowledge of political issues and outside influences on that person's views.
    B. the relative popularity of liberalism and conservatism and that person's ideological history.
    C. the state of the economy and whether the United States is at war.
    D. the wording of public opinion poll questions and the illusion of saliency.

    A (p. 231)

56. Which of the following is NOT true?
    A. Knowledge of politics increases one's sense of political efficacy.
    B. Knowledgeable citizens are better able to recognize their political interests and act consistently on behalf of them.
    C. People with higher education, income, and occupational status are more likely to know about and be active in politics.
    D. A person's beliefs and opinions cannot be influenced by others.

    D (p. 231)

57. In public-opinion surveys, a sample of the total population
    A. must be at least 50 percent of the targeted population.
    B. need be only 15 percent of the targeted population.
    C. must be representative in that the views of those in the sample must accurately and proportionately reflect the views of the whole population.
    D. must be based on all the registered voters in the targeted population.

    C (p. 237)

58. An important reason that public policy and public opinion may not coincide in the U.S. is that
    A. the American system of government includes arrangements such as an appointed judiciary that can produce policy decisions that may run contrary to prevailing popular sentiment.
    B. the American system of government was not designed to account for public opinion.

C. the American system of government was designed to account for the needs and demands of the elite.
D. American society fears a "tyranny of the majority."

A (p. 244)

TRUE OR FALSE

1. The United States is a nation without political ideologies.

   F (p. 211)

2. Americans are more unified on fundamental political values than citizens of any other Western democracy.

   T (p. 213)

3. American public opinion has been formed in reaction to our past feudal aristocracy.

   F (p. 214)

4. Families, social groups, and schools are important institutions where people are politically socialized.

   T (p. 219)

5. Differences in opinion can be influenced by whether one is a man or a woman.

   T (p. 221)

6. Levels of education have not been shown to have an effect on one's political opinions.

   F (p. 223)

7. Liberal and conservative ideologies are clear and well-defined doctrines of thought.

   F (pp. 228–29)

8. Political ideologies do not always provide us with a clear opinion on particular policies.

   T (p. 229)

9. The illusion of saliency can give politicians the mistaken impression that certain opinions are very important to people.

   T (p. 241)

10. Poll pushing is a trend that has been decreasing over the years.

    F (p. 240)

CHAPTER 7 | The Media

MULTIPLE CHOICE

1. Which of the following news sources reaches the most Americans?
   A. radio
   B. television
   C. the Internet
   D. newspapers

   B (p. 252)

2. Which of the following sources of news typically covers topics with the least depth of coverage?
   A. radio
   B. television
   C. the Internet
   D. newspapers

   B (p. 252)

3. Why does news radio repeat stories so often throughout the day?
   A. People need to hear stories more than once for them to sink in.
   B. Most radio listeners listen in their car, so the audience is constantly changing.
   C. There is not enough news to fill an entire day's worth of programming.
   D. Most radio news comes directly from the television script, which is more headlines than in-depth coverage.

   B (p. 254)

4. Which of the following statements is correct?
   A. The national news reporters are generally more favorable to politicians than are local reporters, who have less access.
   B. Local news broadcasters are usually more critical of politicians than are national reporters
   C. Local news reporters are inclined to give politicians more positive coverage than national reporters.
   D. Studies have indicated that in the past decade there is little difference in coverage between local and national reporters.

   C (pp. 253–54)

5. Which group has had great popularity on radio talk shows?
   A. conservatives
   B. liberals
   C. racial and ethnic minorities
   D. All of the above have had great popularity on talk radio.

   A (p. 254)

6. According to the textbook, which of the following is the most important, but not the most popular, source for news?
   A. radio
   B. television
   C. the Internet
   D. newspapers

   D (p. 254)

7. All of the following are reasons why newspaper reportage is critical EXCEPT
   A. most important stories have been broken by newspaper reporters.
   B. political, social, and economic elites rely most heavily on newspapers.
   C. newspapers are the cheapest source of news.
   D. broadcast media do very little original reporting.

   C (p. 254)

8. What is the main benefit of news coverage on the Internet?
   A. It is accessible to more people than any other media source, except for television.
   B. It is the most accurate source of news.
   C. It combines the depth of newspapers with the timeliness of television and radio.
   D. It is the least expensive source of news.

   C (p. 254)

9. The nationalization of news in the United States has had an important political consequence in that
   A. the federal government can now control what every American sees and hears.
   B. Americans are exposed to the same concerns and perspectives and so tend to see the world in similar ways.
   C. The states are now better able to influence government decision-making.
   D. Americans now have a greater ability to influence government decision-making.

   B (p. 262)

10. What percentage of daily newspapers are owned by large media conglomerates?
    A. 25 percent
    B. 40 percent
    C. 55 percent
    D. 75 percent

    D (p. 256)

11. Most newspapers get their news from
    A. local reporters.
    B. wire services.
    C. the Internet.
    D. government reports, press briefings, and announcements.

    B (p. 256)

12. Which of the following is NOT a national newspaper?
    A. *Wall Street Journal*
    B. *Christian Science Monitor*
    C. *Newsweek*
    D. *USA Today*

    C (p. 256)

13. What event dramatically increased the importance of Cable News Network (CNN)?
    A. the Iran-Contra hearings
    B. the Persian Gulf War of 1991
    C. the Los Angeles riots of 1992
    D. the Clinton-Lewinsky scandal

    B (p. 260)

The Media | 83

14. Which of the following statements concerning Internet news is correct?
    A. The Internet has failed to expand the number of news sources, because it relies largely on electronic versions of printed media.
    B. The Internet has greatly expanded the number of different news sources available, beyond the print media.
    C. The Internet has lowered the quality of news reporting, due to the lack of reliable fact checking.
    D. The Internet as a news source is much more biased against the government than is the print media.

    A (p. 260)

15. What trend has helped hasten the homogenization of national news in the past decade?
    A. the rise of the Internet as a major source of news reporting
    B. the growing level of government censorship and restrictions on the media
    C. the corporate consolidation of news media into a small number of conglomerates
    D. the increasing popularity of AM talk radio shows

    C (p. 261)

16. The development of media giants with many different types of media holdings raises the question of whether
    A. local newspapers are perhaps no longer a viable source of news.
    B. the level of censorship and manipulation by the federal government of news media will increase.
    C. there is enough competition among the media to produce a diverse set of views and opinions.
    D. there is a large enough audience for all of the new media sources that have proliferated in the past decade.

    C (p. 261)

17. The term "nationalization of the news" refers to
    A. the decline of local news reporting or public interest in local news.
    B. the fact that more Americans throughout the country are receiving the same news stories.
    C. the greater level of government control and regulation of the news media.
    D. All of the above.

    B (p. 261)

18. What is a news enclave?
    A. a group that seeks special information not provided by the mainstream media
    B. those powerful groups which get their news from the *New York Times* and other elite media
    C. those Americans who do not read, listen, or watch news on a regular basis
    D. a peak in news consumption that immediately follows a major news story

    A (p. 262)

19. Which of the following is the best example of a source for a news enclave?
    A. the *New York Times*
    B. Public Broadcasting System (PBS)
    C. People's Radio Network
    D. *60 Minutes*

    C (p. 262)

20. Which media technology is the most useful for news enclaves?
    A. radio
    B. television
    C. the Internet
    D. newspapers

    C (p. 262)

21. Which of the following best describes the relationship between the government and the media in the United States today?
    A. The government controls most of the media content through regulations and tightly controlled press briefings.
    B. The government owns, but does not control, the major sources of media.
    C. The government does not own but regulates the content and the ownership of broadcast media.
    D. Broadcast media are not regulated in the United States.

    C (p. 255)

22. Which of the following is free-est of government regulation?
    A. newspapers
    B. television
    C. radio
    D. All are equally regulated by the government.

    A (p. 255)

23. Broadcast media are regulated by the
    A. Federal Bureau of Investigation.
    B. Federal Communications Commission.
    C. Public Broadcast System.
    D. Voice of America.

    B (p. 255)

24. The Telecommunications Act of 1996 did all of the following EXCEPT
    A. loosen federal restrictions of media ownership.
    B. allow broadcasters, telephone companies, and cable companies to compete with one another.
    C. make it illegal to make indecent sexual material accessible to minors on the Internet.
    D. All of the following were parts of the act.

    D (p. 255)

25. The _____ requires broadcasters to provide all candidates for the same political office the same opportunity to communicate their message.
    A. right of rebuttal rule
    B. equal time rule
    C. fairness doctrine
    D. diversity in the media doctrine

    B (p. 255)

26. The Supreme Court case *Red Lion Broadcasting Company v. FCC* upheld
    A. the fairness doctrine.
    B. the right of rebuttal.
    C. the equal time rule.
    D. All of the above.

    B (p. 256)

27. If a television station sold commercial time to a Republican candidate for governor but refused to sell time to the Democratic candidate for governor, this would be a violation of
    A. the Telecommunications Act of 1996.
    B. the fairness doctrine.
    C. the equal time rule.
    D. the right of rebuttal.

    C (p. 255)

28. In 1985, the federal government stopped enforcing the _____, arguing that it was no longer necessary due to the increasing number of television and radio stations.
    A. fairness doctrine
    B. right of rebuttal
    C. equal time rule
    D. Children's Programming Act of 1966

    A (p. 256)

29. Which of the following is NOT a significant factor determining the particular interpretation of a news story?
    A. government regulation
    B. the news audience
    C. the sources of the news
    D. the journalists

    A (p. 263)

30. In 1898, the newspaper stories of publisher William Randolph Hearst led to
    A. the development of the first set of government regulations of print media.
    B. a war between the United States and Spain.
    C. World War I.
    D. the development of the wire service.

    B (p. 263)

31. Most newspaper reporters identify themselves as
    A. liberal to moderate.
    B. moderate to conservative.
    C. moderate.
    D. nonpolitical.

    A (p. 263)

32. Which of the following is not a conservative news source?
    A. the *Washington Times*
    B. the *American Spectator*
    C. the *Washington Post*
    D. the *Wall Street Journal*

    C (p. 263)

33. Which of the following is a conservative news broadcast service?
    A. *ABC Nightly News*
    B. *60 Minutes*

C. *Fox News*
D. CNN

C (p. 264)

34. The most important selection bias in news is
    A. the ideology of the journalists.
    B. the audience appeal of a story.
    C. the newsworthiness of a story.
    D. the economic interests of the media's owners.

    B (p. 264)

35. News leaks are useful for all of the following reasons EXCEPT
    A. they help in the cultivation of good relations with the media.
    B. they allow a particular person or group to bolster their positions with opponents.
    C. they are the only legal way to get around most secrecy in government rules.
    D. they allow politicians to speak without attribution.

    C (p. 264)

36. A short, attention-grabbing phrase that summarizes a position is called a
    A. precis.
    B. spin.
    C. sound bite.
    D. news nugget.

    C (p. 265)

37. The news media are most responsive to what segment of the population?
    A. youth.
    B. the affluent.
    C. the elderly.
    D. women.

    B (p. 265)

38. Why are staged protests and conflicts a good way to get one's views publicized?
    A. The audience likes to watch news for its entertainment value, so the media will report the event.
    B. The issues that lead to conflict are likely to be newsworthy.
    C. Protests are easy to report, leading to their frequent appearances in the news.
    D. The U.S. government pays attention to large and violent protests.

    A (p. 266)

88 | Chapter 7

39. What is the chief problem with protest as a media technique?
    A. The protesters are not in control of how their events are interpreted.
    B. Too often the protestors cannot control their own event.
    C. Americans don't like to see political conflict.
    D. Negative publicity often leads to government crackdown.

    A (p. 266)

40. In which of the following events did the media NOT play a central role?
    A. the Korean War
    B. the Vietnam War
    C. the Civil rights movement
    D. Watergate

    A (p. 267)

41. The power of the media to bring public attention to particular issues and problems is called
    A. framing.
    B. canvasing.
    C. agenda setting.
    D. polling.

    C (p. 267)

42. The question of which party was to blame for the shutdown of government services in 1995–96 reveals the important media power of
    A. agenda setting.
    B. framing.
    C. sound bites.
    D. news enclaves.

    B (p. 269)

43. When media coverage effects the way the public evaluates a political leader in future actions, this effect is called
    A. framing.
    B. spinning.
    C. logrolling.
    D. priming.

    D (p. 270)

44. When the media focus on a candidate's relative standing in the polls, rather than on substantive issues, this is called _____ coverage.
    A. bandwagon
    B. horse race

C. momentum
D. lame duck

B (p. 273)

45. During the nineteenth century, newspapers were controlled by
    A. Wall Street.
    B. political parties.
    C. churches and other religious groups.
    D. state governments.

    B (p. 274)

46. Who was the first president to make extensive use of broadcast media in order to build a personal connection with the American people?
    A. Abraham Lincoln
    B. Franklin D. Roosevelt
    C. John F. Kennedy
    D. Richard M. Nixon

    B (p. 274)

47. The Vietnam War initiated the growth of _____ journalism.
    A. yellow
    B. advocacy
    C. adversarial
    D. corporate driven

    C (p. 275)

48. A free media is necessary for popular government for all of the following reasons, EXCEPT
    A. voters need information to make informed choices at the polls.
    B. without the media, citizens would have no knowledge of government actions, other than what the government chose to reveal.
    C. the media brings to light aspects of government policies and actions that would otherwise be known only to insiders with technical knowledge.
    D. All of the above.

    D (p. 276)

49. Which of the following has made politicians more dependent on favorable media coverage?
    A. the decline in political party organizations
    B. the growing popularity of television
    C. divided government
    D. the declining rate of incumbency

    A (p. 276)

50. By 2001, _____ people lived in a country that possessed what can be considered a free press.
    A. one in a hundred
    B. one in twenty
    C. one in five
    D. one in two

    C (p. 277)

51. Reporters have the ability to significantly influence the news because they
    A. have been trained to think critically and to write well.
    B. generally have a great deal of discretion to interpret stories and so have the opportunity to interject personal views and ideals into their stories.
    C. have more access to newsmakers.
    D. are usually supported by trained staff who can better analyze events than the public.

    B (p. 263)

52. The American print and broadcast media tend to be more responsive to the _____ segments of the audience.
    A. lower-class
    B. poor
    C. downscale
    D. upscale

    D (p. 265)

53. Probably more important than the ideological biases of journalists is their selection biases in favor of news that the media views as
    A. favorable to leaders or issues that it supports.
    B. having a great deal of dramatic or entertainment value.
    C. important for the public to be aware of.
    D. sympathetic to government as a whole.

    B (p. 264)

54. The media frenzy over the Monica Lewinsky scandal is evidence that
    A. the media is not at all liberal.
    B. the conservative media has more influence on public opinion than any other group.
    C. the power of the media is declining.
    D. the media's bias is more oriented to entertainment than ideology.

    D (p. 264)

55. The media can set the political agenda in the U.S. by
    A. identifying an issue as a problem that must be solved.
    B. endorsing a particular political candidate.
    C. only accepting advertising from businesses that are identified as being ideologically correct.
    D. maintaining a strictly nonpartisan approach to news-reporting.

    A (p. 267)

56. The power of the media to influence how events and issues are interpreted is called
    A. agenda setting.
    B. framing.
    C. adversarial journalism.
    D. prime timing.

    B (p. 269)

TRUE OR FALSE

1. Television reaches more Americans than any other single source of news.

   T (p. 252)

2. The Internet has led to a huge expansion in the number of different sources of news reporting.

   F (p. 260)

3. Since the 1980s, the ownership of news media has expanded and fractured into many different hands.

   F (p. 256)

4. The Federal Communication Commission no longer requires broadcasters who air controversial issues to provide time for opposing views.

   T (p. 255)

5. Most journalists describe themselves as conservative or moderate to conservative.

   F (p. 263)

6. Broadcast and print media tend to orient their reporting to issues of interest to the lower middle class.

   F (p. 265)

7. Political protests are often the only way some groups can get media attention to their issues and causes.

   T (p. 266)

8. Because of their dependence on government sources, the news media is unable to set the agenda of debate.

   F (p. 267)

9. Media prophecies on a candidate's momentum in an election often become self-fulfilling.

   T (p. 272)

10. Political parties controlled and subsidized newspapers throughout the nineteenth century.

    T (p. 274)

CHAPTER 8 | Political Participation and Voting

MULTIPLE CHOICE

1. The term "suffrage" refers to
   A. the miseries that come from being unable to vote.
   B. the right to vote.
   C. paying poll taxes.
   D. the right to hold public office.

   B (p. 288)

2. Approximately what percentage of eligible American voters have voted in recent presidential elections?
   A. 30 percent
   B. 50 percent
   C. 65 percent
   D. 75 percent

   B (p. 290)

3. Since the 1960s, the percentage of Americans exercising their right to vote has
   A. increased.
   B. decreased.
   C. stayed statistically level.
   D. decreased in federal elections but increased in local elections.

   B (p. 290)

4. The rioting during the 1999 WTO meeting in Seattle is a reminder that
   A. riots are a rare and unusual occurrence in the United States.
   B. rioting is the only available alternative to voting in the United States today.

C. politically motivated riots have been common in the United States throughout its history.
D. political groups in the Pacific Northwest have a penchant for violence.

C (p. 284)

5. The main problem with voting as a form of political participation is
   A. that citizens cannot communicate very much information by only casting a ballot.
   B. that the electoral system is rigged to favor the status quo.
   C. that voting requires more time and commitment than other forms of political participation.
   D. All of the above.

   A (p. 285)

6. Which of the following is NOT a nonelectoral form of political activity?
   A. protests and riots
   B. lobbying
   C. litigation
   D. All of the above are nonelectoral forms of political activity.

   D (p. 285)

7. What is the main difference between voting and lobbying?
   A. Unlike voting, lobbying involves an attempt to directly influence a government official.
   B. Unlike voting, lobbying is a corrupt and undemocratic form of participation.
   C. Unlike voting, lobbying is something done by most American citizens.
   D. Lobbying is a form of voting done only by members of Congress.

   A (p. 285)

8. When defense contractors produced a series of radio ads in 1999, advertising the need for the F-22 fighter plane, they were engaged in
   A. bribery.
   B. lobbying.
   C. public relations.
   D. protest.

   C (p. 286)

9. Litigation is a form of participation in which people
   A. hire advertising firms to promote causes and policies.
   B. file lawsuits in order to change public policies.
   C. pressure members of legislatures to adopt a particular policy.
   D. send letters or e-mails to government officials.

   B (p. 287)

10. Voting
    A. is the form of participation most heavily favored by the wealthy.
    B. gives ordinary Americans a more equal chance to participate in politics.
    C. requires more knowledge and resources than either litigation or lobbying.
    D. is the most recent form of participation arising in western democracies.

    B (p. 287)

11. During the nineteenth and early twentieth centuries, the criteria for determining eligibility to vote were determined by
    A. the U.S. Constitution.
    B. the federal government.
    C. state governments.
    D. the common law tradition.

    C (p. 288)

12. Throughout American history, which of the following was NOT a common restriction government would place on voting rights?
    A. racial restrictions
    B. property requirements
    C. occupational requirements
    D. residency requirements of long duration

    C (pp. 288–89)

13. The Constitution was amended to allow women the right to vote in all public elections in
    A. 1870.
    B. 1885.
    C. 1920.
    D. 1948.

    C (p. 289)

14. What is a poll tax?
    A. a tax that states would impose on all citizens to pay for public opinion research
    B. a fee the political parties would charge people to become a member and vote in their elections
    C. a tax imposed by state governments to register to vote
    D. a tax women had to pay if they wanted to vote in the nineteenth century

    C (p. 289)

15. The Fifteenth Amendment, passed in 1870, mandated that
    A. states were forbidden from having a poll tax.
    B. no state could prevent the right to vote on account of race.

    C. no state could deny the right to vote on account of gender.
    D. literacy tests were forbidden in federal elections.

    B (p. 289)

16. In 1971, what was the main cause for dropping the legal voting age to eighteen?
    A. Young American citizens effectively organized and protested for the right.
    B. It had been one of the important goals for the civil rights movement.
    C. The Constitution mandated the draft age be the same as the voting age.
    D. Government officials hoped it would lead to a decline in disruptive student protests.

    D (p. 289)

17. The term "turnout" describes the number of people who
    A. register to vote.
    B. actually vote.
    C. vote for the incumbent.
    D. A and B.

    B (p. 290)

18. Differing levels of voter turnout throughout the world can best be explained by
    A. the saliency of the election.
    B. whether voting is mandatory.
    C. the degree of proportional representation.
    D. All of the above.

    D (p. 293)

19. Compared with Western Europe, America has a _____ turnout in elections.
    A. higher
    B. lower
    C. roughly equivalent
    D. not comparable

    B (p. 290)

20. States have made it easier to vote in all of the following ways EXCEPT allowing
    A. a two-week voting period.
    B. mail-in ballots.
    C. Internet voting.
    D. for a no-identification policy at the polls.

    D (p. 303)

21. Which of the following was NOT a critical group pushing for an expansion of civil rights for African Americans?
    A. NAACP
    B. DAR
    C. SNCC
    D. SCLC

    B (p. 294)

22. The civil rights movement of the 1950s and 1960s used all of the following methods of participation EXCEPT
    A. sit-ins and marches.
    B. litigation.
    C. lobbying and political pressure.
    D. the power bloc of southern African American voters.

    D (p. 294)

23. What bloc of voters have recently been called the "sleeping giant"?
    A. African Americans
    B. Latinos
    C. Asian Americans
    D. middle-class whites

    B (p. 295)

24. The political power of Asian Americans has recently been hindered because of the
    A. diversity of national backgrounds and cultures.
    B. political apathy amongst Asian American voters.
    C. disenfranchisement of Asian American voters in the 1990s.
    D. lack of a sufficiently large population for bloc voting.

    A (p. 296)

25. The phenomenon called the "gender gap" refers to the fact that
    A. more women vote for Democrats than men.
    B. more men turn out to vote than women.
    C. in families, it is usually women who determine how the family votes.
    D. more men than women have had their ballot invalidated.

    A (p. 296)

26. Approximately what percentage of senators and representatives in Congress are women?
    A. 5 percent
    B. 13 percent

C. 25 percent
D. 40 percent

B (p. 297)

27. Which of the following best describes the goal of the organization EMILY's List?
    A. Promote the expansion of pro-choice legislation.
    B. Advocate a pro-life position.
    C. Raise money for Democratic women candidates to run for office.
    D. Litigate sex discrimination cases in court.

    C (p. 297)

28. Which of the following statements is correct?
    A. Religion has played an important role in organizing political participation.
    B. Religious groups have played a relatively minor role in politically mobilizing Americans.
    C. Catholics and Protestants in the United States remain deeply divided politically.
    D. Political groups usually attempt to keep religious issues out of politics.

    A (p. 298)

29. Evangelical Protestants are more likely to be associated with
    A. the Republican Party.
    B. the Democratic Party.
    C. the Moral Majority Party.
    D. no party; they are typically nonpartisan.

    A (p. 300)

30. What was the Supreme Court case that ruled prayers in public school unconstitutional?
    A. *Plessy v. Ferguson*
    B. *Engel v. Vitale*
    C. *Roe v. Wade*
    D. *Falwell v. Hustler*

    B (p. 298)

31. The power of the Christian Coalition in the 1990s was due to
    A. its ability to donate large sums of money to candidates.
    B. its success in mobilizing a large grassroots base.
    C. the number of its members who were elected to political office.
    D. All of the above.

    B (p. 300)

98 | Chapter 8

32. Which of the following is NOT a key indicator of one's level of participation?
    A. age
    B. income
    C. geographic region
    D. education

    C (pp. 300–302)

33. What is the most common form of participation taken by young people in the United States?
    A. protest marches
    B. community service voluntarism
    C. voting
    D. lobbying

    B (p. 301)

34. The proportion of young people voting has _____ since 1971.
    A. increased slightly
    B. decreased
    C. remained stable
    D. sharply increased

    B (p. 301)

35. Which of the following characteristics does NOT constitute one's socioeconomic status?
    A. level of income
    B. amount of education
    C. prestige of occupation
    D. level of political participation

    D (p. 302)

36. What tendency of Americans did the nineteenth-century writer Alexis de Tocqueville identify as distinctive of our democratic culture?
    A. the tendency to vote at high rates
    B. the tendency to form associations
    C. the tendency to protest policies through riots and other forms of violence
    D. the tendency to shun politics whenever possible

    B (p. 306)

37. Participation in politics depends on
    A. resources, civil engagement, and recruitment.
    B. a good reputation, a high education, and the support of an association.

C. civic spirit, popularity, and energy.
D. lawyers, guns, and money.

A (p. 306)

38. What are white primaries?
    A. primaries held after corrupt practices like the poll tax were outlawed by the Progressives
    B. primaries held in the South that were run by private political parties that excluded African Americans from membership
    C. primaries that are open to everyone, no matter which party one belongs to
    D. primaries that banned Asian Americans from voting in the late nineteenth century

    B (p. 306)

39. What was the original purpose of voter registration?
    A. to reduce corruption by making it more difficult to vote
    B. to simplify the process of voting
    C. to make voters more dependent on the political parties
    D. to raise revenues for the government

    A (p. 308)

40. What was the effect of the Motor Voter Registration Act?
    A. Voter registration rose, but voter turnout did not.
    B. Both voter registration and voter turnout rose.
    C. Neither voter registration nor voter turnout rose.
    D. Voter registration did not rise, but voter turnout levels did.

    A (p. 309)

41. Which of the following statements about voting rights is correct?
    A. Most states have laws restricting the voting rights of persons convicted of felonies.
    B. Laws passed by Congress prevent any abridgement of the voting rights of felons.
    C. The Supreme Court has interpreted the Constitution as preventing one's status as a felon from limiting one's right to vote.
    D. Prison inmates cannot vote, but federal law prevents states from preventing ex-cons from voting.

    A (p. 308)

100 | Chapter 8

42. Studies show that people are more likely to participate in politics when
   A. they are paid to do so.
   B. they believe their input will make a difference.
   C. government officials officially invite input and feedback.
   D. they are able to participate electronically, through e-mail and computer voting.

   B (p. 310)

43. Political _____ is the process by which large numbers of people are organized for political action.
   A. socialization
   B. mobilization
   C. saliency
   D. citizenship

   B (p. 310)

44. Which of the following have political parties been doing less of in recent years?
   A. fund-raising
   B. advertising
   C. mobilizing voters
   D. nominating candidates

   C (p. 312)

45. What have studies shown to be the key element of successful mobilization efforts?
   A. personal contact
   B. direct mailings
   C. extensive use of phone banks
   D. advertising in local media

   A (p. 310)

46. A political institution can best be defined as
   A. a body of the government established by the Constitution.
   B. a set of values and beliefs about what the goals of government should be.
   C. a bureaucracy meant to implement laws passed by the legislature.
   D. any organization that connects people to politics.

   D (p. 313)

47. Checkbook democracy arises when
   A. there is a decline in political participation.
   B. fund raising becomes the most important task for political organizations.

C. participation levels take on an unequal economic bias.
   D. All of the above.

   D (p. 313)

48. The Supreme Court has ruled that
    A. excessive campaign contributions may corrupt the electoral process and may be strongly regulated by Congress.
    B. campaign contributions are a form of free speech.
    C. it is illegal for a candidate to spend more than $10,000 of her or his own money to run for office.
    D. The Supreme Court has remained silent on the issue of campaign contributions.

    B (p. 313)

49. If you are a U.S. citizen, aged eighteen or older, what is required for you to vote?
    A. You must register with the government.
    B. You must be photographed and fingerprinted.
    C. You must go through a brief background check to make sure you have no criminal record.
    D. All of the above.

    A (p. 314)

50. Which of the following was NOT a response Americans had to 9/11?
    A. Monetary donations to charities increased.
    B. Interest in government jobs spread.
    C. Critical debate arose concerning domestic security laws.
    D. Distrust in the government grew.

    D (p. 307)

51. The explanation for political participation that points to the characteristics of individuals focuses on
    A. socioeconomic status.
    B. membership in social organizations.
    C. formal obstacles like the poll tax or white primary.
    D. mobilization by political institutions.

    A (p. 302)

52. The socioeconomic status model explains political participation by examining an individual's
    A. level of education, income, and occupational status.
    B. membership in community organizations.
    C. legal right to vote.
    D. membership in political organizations.

    A (p. 302)

53. Which of the following about political participation is true?
    A. African Americans and Latinos are less likely to participate in politics than whites.
    B. African Americans and Latinos participate in politics at the same or higher levels than whites.
    C. African Americans hardly participate in politics at all, while Latinos participate at extraordinarily high levels.
    D. Latinos barely participate at all in politics, while African Americans participate at extraordinarily high levels.

    A (p. 302)

54. Which of the following about political participation is true?
    A. Young people are far less likely to participate in politics than older people.
    B. Older people are far less likely to participate in politics than younger people.
    C. Young people are equally as likely to participate in politics as older people.
    D. Neither young people nor older people participate much in politics.

    A (p. 302)

55. The strongest critique of the socioeconomic status model for explaining political participation is that
    A. African Americans with high levels of education do not participate.
    B. education levels are rising while rates of participation are falling.
    C. people from the lowest income brackets participate in politics the most.
    D. income levels are decreasing while rates of political participation are increasing.

    B (p. 302)

56. An example of the way in which the social setting can influence political participation is that in the United States, _____ help foster political participation.
    A. Vietnam veterans' groups
    B. bowling leagues
    C. churches
    D. workplace cooperatives

    C (p. 302)

TRUE OR FALSE

1. Rioting has been a recent and rare form of political activity in the United States.

    F (p. 284)

2. Participation in elections has been declining over the years.

    T (p. 284)

3. Voting is the only form of political participation open to most Americans.

    F (p. 284)

4. Many states used to have property requirements for those wanting to vote.

    T (p. 288)

5. Poll taxes and literacy tests were used by southern states to prevent African Americans from voting.

    T (p. 289)

6. Suffragettes were women protesting for the right to vote.

    T (p. 289)

7. The Southern Christian Leadership Conference (SCLC) led the organized protests against the civil rights movement and desegregation.

    F (p. 294)

8. Women are more likely than men to vote for Republicans.

    F (p. 296)

9. Voter registration was instituted to make it harder to vote.

    T (p. 308)

10. Recently, political parties have spent more effort at mobilizing voters than previously.

    F (p. 312)

CHAPTER 9 | Political Parties

MULTIPLE CHOICE

1. Which famous American, in his farewell address, encouraged his fellow citizens to shun partisan politics?
   A. Alexander Hamilton
   B. Thomas Jefferson
   C. George Washington
   D. George Mason

   C (p. 321)

2. Which of the following provides the best description of political parties?
   A. organizations that influence government through fund-raising
   B. organizations that are established by the Constitution to nominate candidates
   C. organizations that try to influence government by getting their members elected to office
   D. organizations that, until the twentieth century, were considered seditious

   C (p. 322)

3. Which of the following explains why the organizational structure of political parties looks like it does?
   A. the structure of the American electoral system
   B. the organizational shape of interest groups, which parties were patterned after
   C. the growth of big business
   D. the role of the media in publicizing politics

   A (p. 323)

Political Parties | 105

4. Which of the following statements is correct?
   A. The United States has stronger parties than most European democracies.
   B. European democracies tend to have stronger parties than the United States.
   C. Western Europe does not have formal political parties comparable with those of the United States.
   D. The parties in the United States are the descendants of eighteenth-century English parties.

   B (p. 323)

5. Within the government itself, parties are
   A. relatively unimportant, except in election years.
   B. stable coalitions of individuals with shared or overlapping interests.
   C. necessary for propagating official ideology.
   D. important for ideological identification but not useful for actually initiating public policy.

   B (p. 323)

6. Beginning in the late eighteenth century, the United States began a tradition of
   A. single-party mandate.
   B. two-party system.
   C. multiple-party system.
   D. proportional representation.

   B (p. 323)

7. The establishment of the Republican Party is a good example of
   A. external mobilization.
   B. internal mobilization.
   C. seditious mobilization.
   D. elite bargaining.

   A (p. 324)

8. Internal mobilization occurs when
   A. conflicts within government break out and the factions try to mobilize popular support.
   B. party leaders try to rally support for their platforms once they are in government.
   C. citizens who are deemed to be undesirable outsiders are excluded from the party.
   D. all the funds a party spends come from soft money.

   A (p. 324)

9. Which of the following parties did NOT originate through internal mobilization?
   A. Jeffersonians
   B. Federalists
   C. Republicans
   D. All of the above were formed through internal mobilization.

   C (p. 324)

10. Who was the founder of the Democratic Party?
    A. George Washington
    B. Alexander Hamilton
    C. Andrew Jackson
    D. Abraham Lincoln

    C (p. 324)

11. During the middle to late nineteenth century, the Democratic Party was divided by
    A. slavery and the Civil War.
    B. fiscal policy during the tariff crisis.
    C. lingering conflict concerning the War of 1812.
    D. westward expansion of the United States.

    A (p. 326)

12. Which of the following groups was NOT part of the New Deal coalition?
    A. Catholics
    B. Farmers
    C. business leaders
    D. organized labor

    C (p. 327)

13. The New Deal coalition was broken up by
    A. Dwight Eisenhower.
    B. the movement of conservative southerners to the Republican Party.
    C. the end of the Great Depression at the beginning of World War II.
    D. the "triangulated" positions of Bill Clinton.

    B (pp. 327–28)

14. Bill Clinton's policy of _____ was based on his desire to position himself between conservative Republicans and liberal Democrats.
    A. compassionate conservatism
    B. triangulation
    C. internal mobilization
    D. electoral realignment

    B (p. 328)

15. Who was the first presidential candidate of the Republican Party?
    A. Andrew Jackson
    B. John Fremont
    C. Abraham Lincoln
    D. Ulysses Grant

    B (p. 328)

16. In the years after the Civil War until the 1930s, the _____ were the dominant party in the United States.
    A. Republicans
    B. Democrats
    C. Whigs
    D. Progressives

    A (p. 330)

17. Which of the following events occurred in 1994?
    A. The Republican Party won control of both houses of Congress for the first time since the 1950s.
    B. The Republican Party lost control of the Senate for the first time in twenty years.
    C. Bill Clinton won his second term in office, defeating Bob Dole.
    D. House Speaker Newt Gingrich resigned his seat after the Republican Party suffered severe losses.

    A (p. 331)

18. When a party that has dominated national politics for a lengthy period is replaced by another party, which itself becomes dominant, this event is called
    A. an electoral realignment.
    B. proportional representation.
    C. divided government.
    D. external mobilization.

    A (p. 331)

19. When the presidency is controlled by one party, and one or both houses of Congress are controlled by another party, this situation is called
    A. electoral realignment.
    B. divided government.
    C. seditious government.
    D. internal mobilization.

    B (p. 332)

20. Which of the following was NOT a date of an electoral realignment?
    A. 1800
    B. 1828
    C. 1932
    D. 1994

    D (pp. 331–32)

21. Since the 1960s, American national politics can best be described as
    A. divided government.
    B. Republican hegemony.
    C. Democrat dominance.
    D. sectionalist.

    A (p. 332)

22. All of the following are prerequisites of an electoral realignment EXCEPT
    A. the appearance of new issues or problems.
    B. the creation of a new party.
    C. the existence of an economic or political crisis.
    D. a permanent shift in partisan loyalties or many voters.

    B (p. 332)

23. Which of the following statements concerning third parties is FALSE?
    A. Third parties are often short lived.
    B. Successful third parties often have their programs adopted by one of the two major parties.
    C. The earliest third parties in the United States arose as a result of the Great Depression.
    D. Third parties often have support limited by geographic region.

    C (pp. 333–34)

24. As a third-party candidate, Ross Perot captured approximately _____ percent of the popular vote in the 1992 presidential election.
    A. 5
    B. 10
    C. 20
    D. 30

    C (p. 333)

25. One important cause of the United States's two-party system is
    A. the Constitution's requirement for bipartisanship in Congress.
    B. single-member electoral districts.
    C. multimember electoral districts.
    D. proportional representation.

    B (p. 336)

26. When the winner of an electoral race is the one who gets more votes than any other candidate, this is known as
    A. the majority system.
    B. the plurality system.
    C. proportional representation.
    D. the winner take all system.

    B (p. 337)

27. Third-party candidates are better off under what system of election?
    A. majority system
    B. plurality system
    C. proportional representation
    D. None of these systems is favorable to third parties.

    C (p. 337)

28. How often do the major political parties have a national convention?
    A. twice a year
    B. once a year
    C. once every two years
    D. once every four years

    D (p. 337)

29. Which of the following is NOT accomplished at a party's national convention?
    A. nominating the presidential and vice presidential candidate
    B. determining the parties rules and bylaws
    C. developing and ratifying the parties platform
    D. nominating Senate and House candidates

    D (p. 337)

30. A closed meeting of a political group's members, in order to determine strategy and select candidates, is called a
    A. convention.
    B. caucus.
    C. party.
    D. district.

    B (p. 337)

31. A party's _____ contains its philosophy, principles, and policy positions.
    A. caucus
    B. convention
    C. platform
    D. machine

    C (p. 341)

32. Which of the following is NOT a function of a party's national committee?
   A. raising funds
   B. resolving disputes between factions of the party
   C. selecting presidential and vice-presidential candidates
   D. enhancing the media image of the party

   C (p. 341)

33. Who elects the chairperson for the Republicans' and Democrats' national committees?
   A. the party members
   B. the delegates to the national convention
   C. the president if the party controls the White House, and the party committee if the party does not control the White House
   D. the chairperson of the committee who appoints a successor

   C (p. 341)

34. A party's platform is best understood as
   A. a negotiated agreement between the party's various factions.
   B. a public relations program designed for media consumption.
   C. a clear statement of the principles to which each party candidate will be committed.
   D. a contract with the American people.

   A (p. 341)

35. The power of _____ means that political party bosses can confer governmental favors on loyal party members.
   A. machines
   B. patronage
   C. soft money
   D. caucuses

   B (p. 344)

36. During the era of political machines, what was the most common favor political bosses distributed to loyal party members?
   A. money
   B. jobs
   C. patents
   D. tariffs

   B (p. 344)

37. Strong, often corrupt, urban political party organizations during the late nineteenth and early twentieth centuries were called
   A. gangs.
   B. juntas.

C. machines.
D. corporations.

C (p. 344)

38. State and local party organizations do all of the following EXCEPT
    A. raise funds for candidates.
    B. conduct voter registration drives.
    C. litigate against unfavorable policies.
    D. recruit candidates for office.

    C (p. 344)

39. Which of the following is the best definition of soft money?
    A. money collected through illegal donations
    B. money contributed to a party to offset the cost of internal organization and voter registration but not spent on a candidate's election
    C. nonmonetary donations to a party, such as use of airplanes and hotel rooms, which are not officially considered income
    D. money that is left over after the election

    B (p. 345)

40. An individual's psychological attachment to one party or another is called a party
    A. ideology.
    B. opinion.
    C. identification.
    D. tradition.

    C (p. 345)

41. Partisan ties in the United States have _____ in recent years.
    A. originated
    B. increased
    C. declined
    D. been steady

    C (p. 345)

42. If a citizen not only votes for a party but donates time, money, and effort to party affairs, they are known as a party
    A. ideologue.
    B. boss.
    C. activist.
    D. volunteer.

    C (p. 345)

43. Since the 1930s, African Americans' party identification has been overwhelmingly
    A. Republican.
    B. Democratic.
    C. nonpartisan.
    D. Independent.

    B (p. 346)

44. Which of the following are most likely to support the Republican Party?
    A. Latinos
    B. women
    C. the wealthy
    D. Jewish Americans

    C (p. 347)

45. One of the most difficult tasks recently for political parties has been
    A. fund-raising.
    B. voter registration.
    C. candidate recruitment.
    D. media strategy.

    C (p. 348)

46. Which of the following congressional procedures is dependent on partisanship?
    A. election of the Speaker of the House
    B. committee assignments
    C. A and B
    D. None of the above.

    C (p. 352)

47. Historically, political parties have been most useful for _____ to achieve political power.
    A. the wealthy
    B. conservatives
    C. the poor and working class
    D. rural voters

    C (p. 354)

48. Vigorous political parties _____ voter turnout.
    A. depress
    B. promote

C. subvert
D. corrupt

B (p. 356)

49. Strong parties may provide an important link between government and
    A. interest groups.
    B. money.
    C. churches
    D. democratic participation.

    D (p. 357)

50. One proposal suggested by the authors for making political parties stronger and more responsible is
    A. to make parties more responsible for the bulk of campaign financing.
    B. to make parties more ideological, like those in western Europe.
    C. to revive the urban political machines of the last century.
    D. to move the United States toward proportional representation.

    A (p. 358)

51. Throughout its history, American politics has been dominated by
    A. one major political party.
    B. two major political parties.
    C. three major political parties.
    D. four major political parties.

    B (p. 324)

52. From 1828 to 1860, the _____ Party was the dominant force in American politics.
    A. Communist
    B. Democratic
    C. Federalist
    D. Republican

    B (p. 324)

53. The _____ ended the dominance of the Democratic Party until its resurgence in the 1930s.
    A. Whiskey Rebellion
    B. war with Mexico
    C. Civil War
    D. cold war

    C (p. 326)

114 | Chapter 9

54. Contemporary support for the Democratic Party comes primarily from
    A. America's corporate elite, African Americans, midwesterners, and the military.
    B. veterans groups, environmentalists, Christian fundamentalists, and anti-abortion activists.
    C. anti-gun control advocates, feminists, millenarians, and federal bureaucrats.
    D. African Americans, women, federal bureaucrats, and the nonprofit sector of the economy.

    D (p. 328)

55. The _____ ended the dominance of the Republican Party.
    A. Great Depression
    B. First World War
    C. Teapot Dome scandal
    D. Credit Mobilier scandal

    A (p. 330)

56. A realignment in the relative power of America's major political parties occurs when
    A. a large influx of immigration to the United States upsets the existing political balance and causes social turmoil until the political parties persuade the newcomers to support their programs.
    B. a president is impeached or resigns from office.
    C. new issues combined with economic or political crises persuade large numbers of voters to reexamine their traditional partisan loyalties and permanently shift their support from one party to another.
    D. a new amendment is added to the U.S. Constitution.

    C (p. 331)

57. There is general agreement among political scientists that _____ electoral realignments have occurred in American political history.
    A. two
    B. five
    C. twelve
    D. forty-two

    B (p. 331)

58. In the United States, third parties typically represent
    A. the interests of women.
    B. extremist religious groups.
    C. the political interests of America's allies, who, because the policies of the U.S. could affect their futures, attempt to influence the American decision-making process.

D. social and economic protests that, for one or another reason, are not given voice by the two major parties.

D (p. 333)

59. A key factor in stimulating Americans to vote is
    A. competition between political parties.
    B. nominating candidates to office who are physically attractive.
    C. providing them with enough of a financial incentive to go to the polls.
    D. a virtual bombardment of political advertising.

    A (p. 356)

60. Party identification occurs when
    A. individual voters form strong psychological ties to a political party.
    B. individuals attend the convention of a particular political party.
    C. a political organization files an official name with the Federal Elections Commission.
    D. the national news media assigns a particular title to a political organization.

    A (p. 345)

61. A party activist is an individual who
    A. attends every social function that a political party stages.
    B. writes favorable news reports for the national media.
    C. commits acts of civil disobedience when asked by a political party.
    D. not only votes, but who also contributes time, energy, effort, and financial resources to party affairs.

    D (p. 345)

62. Women in the United States are _____ the _____ Party.
    A. overwhelmingly committed to; Republican
    B. somewhat more likely to support; Republican
    C. overwhelmingly committed to; Democratic
    D. somewhat more likely to; Democratic

    D (p. 346)

63. Men in the United States are _____ the _____ Party.
    A. overwhelmingly committed to; Republican
    B. somewhat more likely to support; Republican
    C. overwhelmingly committed to; Democratic
    D. somewhat more likely to; Democratic

    B (p. 346)

64. Between the Civil War and the 1960s, the _____ was a Democratic stronghold.
    A. Midwest
    B. West
    C. South
    D. Southwest

    C (p. 347)

65. In contemporary American politics, support for the Republican Party comes from the
    A. South, West, and Southwest.
    B. South, Northeast, and Midwest.
    C. Northeast, Midwest, and West.
    D. Northeast, Midwest, and Southwest.

    A (p. 347)

66. Which of the following is NOT an important principle of responsible party government?
    A. Parties should allow candidates to run their own campaigns.
    B. Parties should develop a coherent set of campaign issues.
    C. Parties should mobilize voters.
    D. Parties should fulfill their campaign promises once in office.

    A (p. 357)

TRUE OR FALSE

1. The shape of American political party organizations depends on the shape of the American electoral process.

   T (p. 323)

2. The first political parties in the United States were the Democrats and Republicans.

   F (p. 324)

3. The Republican Party was created around the issues of antislavery and commercial growth.

   T (p. 329)

4. The Republicans have controlled the House of Representatives since the 1950s.

   F (p. 330)

5. There have been at least five electoral realignments in U.S. history.

   T (p. 331)

6. Most third parties in the United States today had their origin in the nineteenth century.

   F (p. 335)

7. Most electoral districts in the United States are multimember districts.

   F (p. 336)

8. The national committee of each of the major parties is responsible for nominating their party's candidates for all federal offices.

   F (pp. 337, 341)

9. Women are more likely to vote for the Democratic Party than men are.

   T (p. 346)

10. Strong political parties decrease voter turnout.

    F (p. 356)

CHAPTER 10 | Campaigns and Elections

MULTIPLE CHOICE

1. What is the main difference between elections in a democracy and elections under an authoritarian regime?
   A. In democracies, elections are about issues, while under authoritarian governments, elections concern the personalities of leaders.
   B. Democratic regimes allow for viable opposition, while the leaders do not permit themselves to lose under an authoritarian government.
   C. Unlike democracies, there are no political parties in an authoritarian regime.
   D. Authoritarian regimes never have elections.

   B (p. 365)

2. _____ is another name for the right to vote.
   A. Representation
   B. Suffrage
   C. Gerrymander
   D. Incumbent

   B (p. 366)

3. What is the function of an election in a democracy?
   A. It promotes accountability among the leaders.
   B. It helps to politically protect different groups in society.
   C. It serves to legitimate the government.
   D. All of the above.

   D (p. 366)

4. When are national elections held in the United States?
   A. the first Tuesday of November every year
   B. the first Tuesday of November every other year
   C. the first Tuesday of November every four years
   D. None of the above.

   B (p. 367)

5. When a congressional election is held that does not coincide with a presidential election, it is called a
   A. primary election.
   B. franchise vote.
   C. midterm election.
   D. referendum.

   C (p. 367)

6. The primary responsibility for conducting public elections rests with
   A. the federal government.
   B. state and local governments.
   C. political parties.
   D. the candidates running for office.

   B (p. 367)

7. In order for a political party to select a candidate to run in the general election, it holds a
   A. primary election.
   B. referendum.
   C. midterm election.
   D. franchise vote.

   A (p. 367)

8. If a voter must be registered with a party prior to voting in the party's election, this is called
   A. an open primary.
   B. a closed primary.
   C. a majority system.
   D. an Australian ballot.

   B (pp. 367–68)

9. What is a referendum?
   A. It is the congressional election held between presidential elections.
   B. It is the right and power to vote.
   C. It is the practice of voting directly for proposed laws.
   D. It is the process by which a party selects its candidates for the general election.

   C (p. 368)

10. Which of the following is the best example of direct democracy in practice in the United States?
    A. gerrymandering
    B. retrospective voting
    C. referendum
    D. issue advocacy

    C (p. 368)

11. If the winner of an election is whoever receives the most votes, regardless of the percentage of votes received, the candidate has been running under a _____ system
    A. majority
    B. plurality
    C. proportionality
    D. unitary

    B (p. 368)

12. Most European nations employ what system of elections?
    A. majority
    B. plurality system
    C. proportional representation
    D. Most European nations do not elect representatives.

    C (p. 368)

13. _____ is the most common electoral system used in general elections in the United States.
    A. The majority system
    B. The plurality system
    C. The proportional representation system
    D. The gerrymandered system

    B (p. 368)

14. Smaller and weaker parties are most likely to have electoral success under which system of elections?
    A. the proportional representation system
    B. the majority system
    C. the plurality system
    D. the unitary system

    A (p. 368)

15. The boundaries of legislative districts in the United States are redrawn every _____ years.
    A. two
    B. four

C. six
D. ten

D (p. 370)

16. When the Supreme Court announced the principle of "one person one vote," what did it mean?
    A. Voters may only vote once in an election.
    B. Within a state, electoral districts must have roughly equal populations.
    C. No one could be denied suffrage on the basis of race or gender.
    D. Voting was an individual right, not a group right.

    B (p. 370)

17. The practice of _____ means that district boundaries have been purposefully drawn to unfairly advantage one group or party.
    A. proportional representation
    B. gerrymandering
    C. balloting
    D. incumbency

    B (pp. 371–72)

18. When legislatures draw district lines made up largely of underrepresented minority groups, this practice is called
    A. benign gerrymandering.
    B. group redistricting.
    C. split ticketing.
    D. affirmative action.

    A (p. 372)

19. In what case did the Supreme Court say that purposefully drawing districts where the majority were members of a single minority group, in order to ensure minority representation, was not constitutional?
    A. *Reynolds v. Sims*
    B. *Bush v. Gore*
    C. *Shaw v. Reno*
    D. *Brown v. Board of Education*

    C (p. 372)

20. Before the 1890s, who used to be responsible for printing election ballots?
    A. the federal government
    B. state governments
    C. political parties
    D. the National League of Women Voters

    C (p. 372)

122 | Chapter 10

21. If you were to vote for a Republican for president and for a Democrat for senator, you have engaged in
    A. a referendum.
    B. an open primary.
    C. split-ticket voting.
    D. the coattail effect.

    C (p. 372)

22. Split-ticket voting
    A. increases political corruption at the polling booths.
    B. increases partisan divisions in government.
    C. decreases partisan conflict in government.
    D. increases the coattail effect during midterm elections.

    B (p. 372)

23. The _____ is the last example of indirect voting in national elections.
    A. referendum
    B. electoral college
    C. closed primary
    D. franchise

    B (p. 376)

24. If George W. Bush won the plurality of votes in Texas during the 2000 election, and Texas has thirty representatives to Congress, how many electoral votes from Texas did Bush win?
    A. 0
    B. 30
    C. 32
    D. Only the Supreme Court could tell.

    C (p. 376)

25. Which of the following events helped lead to a change in the way that the electoral college chose the president and vice president?
    A. the riots caused by the Alien and Sedition Act, in the 1790s
    B. the duel between Alexander Hamilton and Aaron Burr in 1803
    C. the failure of Andrew Jackson to win the White House in 1824
    D. the succession of southern states in 1860

    B (p. 377)

26. Which of the following presidents succeeded in winning the plurality of the popular vote?
    A. George W. Bush
    B. Rutherford B. Hayes

C. Dwight Eisenhower
   D. Benjamin Harrison

   C (p. 377)

27. Why is it unlikely that the electoral college will be abolished anytime in the near future?
    A. It benefits states in the West and Midwest more than a strict popular vote would.
    B. The major parties worry it might benefit third parties.
    C. Minority voters in urban states feel that their voting strength would be diminished in direct elections.
    D. All of the above.

    D (p. 377)

28. Who is the incumbent?
    A. the current officeholder, running for re-election
    B. the candidate who raises the most money during the campaign
    C. the official candidate for a political party, running in the general elections
    D. the label for whoever is leading in the polls on the day of the election

    A (p. 378)

29. Approximately how much money does it take for a candidate to have a reasonable chance of winning a seat in the House of Representatives?
    A. $50,000
    B. $500,000
    C. $5,000,000
    D. $10,000,000

    B (p. 379)

30. Campaign consultants do all of the following EXCEPT
    A. conduct opinion polls.
    B. organize direct mailings.
    C. develop the issues on which the candidate will focus.
    D. All of the above are tasks of the campaign consultant.

    D (p. 379)

31. When does public opinion polling take place during a campaign?
    A. at the very beginning
    B. only toward the end of the campaign
    C. throughout the entire campaign
    D. Polling is too expensive for any campaign except for the presidency.

    C (pp. 379–80)

124 | Chapter 10

32. Which of the following primary battles is the best example of an ideological clash, rather than a personality clash?
    A. Al Gore and Bill Bradley in 2000
    B. George Bush and John McCain in 2000
    C. George H. W. Bush and Pat Buchanan in 1992
    D. All of the above involved ideological clashes.

    C (p. 381)

33. For their primaries, most but not all state parties use what type of election?
    A. winner takes all
    B. proportional representation
    C. majority rules
    D. the unitary system

    B (p. 383)

34. During the earliest years of the United States, who nominated the candidates for president?
    A. The incumbent president chose both candidates.
    B. Members of the major political parties chose their own nominee.
    C. Nominations were controlled by each party's congressional caucus.
    D. Political machine bosses controlled the entire nominating process.

    C (p. 383)

35. Before the post–World War II era, dark horse candidates were most likely to arise at a national convention when
    A. deadlocks between major factions developed.
    B. no other candidate wanted the nomination.
    C. charismatic leaders dominate the proceedings.
    D. None of the above explain why dark horse candidates arise.

    A (p. 384)

36. Party activists who are elected to vote at a party's national convention are called
    A. incumbents.
    B. delegates.
    C. electors.
    D. nominees.

    B (p. 385)

37. Which party has reserved slots at the national convention for elected superdelegates?
    A. the Republicans
    B. the Democrats

    C. the Greens
    D. All parties have superdelegates.

    B (p. 385)

38. Who is the major audience for contemporary national conventions?
    A. party loyalists
    B. the opposing candidates
    C. the mass media
    D. Modern conventions are private caucuses with no audience outside the delegates themselves.

    C (p. 386)

39. In the nineteenth and early twentieth centuries, election campaigns tended to be
    A. capital intensive.
    B. labor intensive.
    C. media driven.
    D. short and peaceful.

    B (p. 386)

40. Which of the following do modern political campaigns NOT depend on?
    A. broadcast media
    B. direct mailings
    C. a large army of volunteers from the party
    D. phone banks

    C (p. 390)

41. What was the legal question before the Supreme Court as a result of the 2000 presidential elections?
    A. Who won the popular vote in Florida?
    B. Was it legal to count overseas ballots that were postmarked after Election Day?
    C. Should Florida continue to manually recount ballots?
    D. Should ballots with hanging chads be counted?

    C (p. 392)

42. What was the vote in the Supreme Court case *Bush v. Gore*?
    A. 9–0
    B. 5–4
    C. 6–3
    D. 8–1

    B (p. 392)

43. What was the main problem with the manner in which Al Gore conducted his presidential campaign?
    A. He was considered too liberal for most centrist voters.
    B. He tried to distance himself too much from Bill Clinton.
    C. He refused across-the-board tax cuts.
    D. All of the above.

    D (pp. 393–96)

44. Private groups that raise and distribute funds for election campaigns are called
    A. corporations.
    B. political parties.
    C. political action committees.
    D. political consulting firms.

    C (p. 399)

45. Why have many political commentators argued that PACs corrupt the political process?
    A. They make candidates overly reliant on their party.
    B. They allow for too much influence for corporations and other well-funded interests by making huge contributions to campaigns.
    C. They do not have to publicly disclose their contributions.
    D. All of the above.

    B (p. 399)

46. The right of candidates to spend their own money on running for office
    A. is limited by a cap of $50 million.
    B. is protected absolutely by the First Amendment, according to the Supreme Court.
    C. was forbidden by the Campaign Reform Act of 1974.
    D. is allowed only if the candidate could meet every personal dollar with a dollar of outside donations.

    B (p. 400)

47. What is a common way for interest groups, corporations, and political parties to aid a candidate while avoiding campaign finance laws?
    A. fund money through the unregulated PACs.
    B. engage in issue advocacy.
    C. use spot advertisements.
    D. All of the above.

    B (p. 400)

48. Which of the following were NOT major contributors to George Bush's 2000 presidential campaign?
    A. airlines

B. trial lawyers
   C. energy producers
   D. tobacco companies

   B (p. 404)

49. Partisan loyalty is likely to be highest in the election of
    A. the president.
    B. a state legislator.
    C. a U.S. senator.
    D. a governor.

    B (p. 406)

50. If a citizen votes for a candidate because he or she approves of the candidate's past record, this is called
    A. prospective voting.
    B. retrospective voting.
    C. poll testing.
    D. ticket splitting.

    B (p. 408)

51. When American voters support only one party's candidates, they are said to be voting a
    A. dual ticket.
    B. single ticket.
    C. straight ticket.
    D. split ticket.

    C (p. 372)

52. The result that is produced when voters cast a ballot for the president and then automatically vote for the remainder of that party's candidates is called the
    A. shirttail effect.
    B. coattail effect.
    C. pocket veto effect.
    D. logrolling effect.

    B (p. 372)

53. A majority electoral system, which is used on a limited basis in the United States, requires that a candidate must win _____ to win an election.
    A. at least 25 percent of all votes cast
    B. at least 40 percent of all votes cast
    C. 50 percent, plus one, of all votes cast
    D. at least 60 percent of all votes cast, plus a percentage of absentee ballots

    C (p. 368)

54. Plurality and majority systems tend to
    A. increase the number of political parties.
    B. decrease the number of political parties.
    C. evolve into single-party systems.
    D. devolve into anarchy.

    B (p. 369)

55. Three types of factors—_____—influence the decisions of voters at the polls.
    A. wealth, education, and issues
    B. advertising, partisan loyalty, and personality
    C. partisan loyalty, issues, and the characteristics of candidates
    D. advertising, debates, and issues

    C (p. 405)

56. Political scientists call voters' choices that focus on future behavior _____, while those based on past performance are called _____.
    A. prospective voting; retrospective voting
    B. retrospective voting; prospective voting
    C. partisan voting; issue voting
    D. issue voting; partisan voting

    A (p. 408)

TRUE OR FALSE

1. The introduction of primary elections was meant to weaken political parties.

   T (p. 367)

2. Some states, but not the national government, allow for referendums.

   T (p. 368)

3. Most national elections in the United States use a system of proportional representation.

   F (p. 368)

4. Denying an individual the right to vote through literacy tests and poll taxes is called gerrymandering.

   F (p. 371)

5. The electoral college cannot elect any candidate who has not also won the popular vote.

   F (p. 377)

6. Incumbents usually have an easier time successfully campaigning for office than nonincumbents.

   T (p. 378)

7. Contemporary campaigns are capital intensive, rather than labor intensive.

   T (p. 390)

8. PACs can make larger campaign contributions than individuals are legally allowed to make.

   T (p. 399)

9. Soft money is money spent by parties on organizational development and voter registration, which is not regulated as campaign expenditures.

   T (p. 398)

10. A voter's partisan loyalty is at its highest in presidential races.

    F (p. 406)

CHAPTER 11 | Groups and Interests

MULTIPLE CHOICE

1. A criticism of interest-group pluralism is
   A. its inherent propensity for compromise, the character of which tends to be anti-democratic.
   B. its class favor in favor of those with greater financial resources.
   C. that its ideals are too closely associated with Marxist-Leninist ideology, and are therefore unacceptable to the majority of Americans.
   D. that it favors the interests of large states over those of small states.

   B (p. 416)

2. The best description of the ideal of pluralism is that
   A. the public good should always trump individual interests.
   B. interests should be free to compete with each other for governmental influence.
   C. interest groups are factions that endanger liberty.
   D. democracy is best served by legalizing but regulating the influence of interest groups.

   B (p. 416)

3. What contemporary political scientists call an interest group, James Madison called a
   A. mob.
   B. faction.
   C. oligarchy.
   D. corporation.

   B (p. 416)

4. Which of the following is NOT a theoretical assumption of pluralism?
   A. All interests are represented.
   B. The result of competition among interests is in the common good.
   C. All groups have equal access to the political process.
   D. Many extreme interest groups need to be banned in the name of the public good.

   D (p. 416)

5. Which of the following is NOT a function of interest groups?
   A. to influence governmental decisions
   B. to lobby government officials
   C. to get their members elected to political office
   D. to educate their members and the public about the issues that affect them

   C (p. 417)

6. The Teamsters and the AFL-CIO are examples of what kind of interest group?
   A. a public interest group
   B. a business group
   C. a labor group
   D. an ideological group

   C (p. 419)

7. The Christian Coalition is best described as a(n) _____ group.
   A. public interest
   B. ideological
   C. labor
   D. professional

   B (p. 419)

8. Successful interest groups quickly become
   A. bureaucratized.
   B. corrupted.
   C. outdated.
   D. rich.

   A (p. 420)

9. Which of the following is NOT a key organizational component of interest groups?
   A. members
   B. money
   C. leadership
   D. newsletter and website

   D (p. 420)

10. When political scientist E. E. Schattschneider said, "The heavenly chorus of interest groups sing with a distinctly upper class accent," he meant that
    A. the interests of the wealthy are more likely to be favored by God.
    B. the theory of pluralism ignores the fact that the wealthy are better organized than the poor.
    C. the way in which certain interests groups communicate often will give away their class interests.
    D. interest goods need to work on harmonizing with each other better.

    B (p. 416)

11. Which of the following groups is most likely to be organized?
    A. single mothers
    B. the homeless
    C. graduate teaching assistants
    D. truck drivers

    D (p. 420)

12. When a group is called a membership association, it means that
    A. the group accepts anyone as a member.
    B. members play an important role in the daily activities of the group.
    C. members vote directly for the leaders.
    D. membership is a mandatory requirement for receiving any of the groups benefits.

    B (p. 421)

13. When paid staff conduct most of the daily business of a group, that group is best described as a
    A. staff organization.
    B. free-rider group.
    C. lobbyist firm.
    D. PAC.

    A (p. 421)

14. A benefit that is sought by an interest group but that once achieved cannot be denied to nonmembers is called a
    A. free rider.
    B. collective good.
    C. right.
    D. solidarity benefit.

    B (p. 421)

15. If one enjoys the benefits of a group's collective efforts but did not contribute to those efforts, one is called a
    A. citizen.

B. subject.
C. free rider.
D. lobbyist.

C (p. 421)

16. When membership in an organization allows for a reduction in the price of museum tickets, this is called a
    A. solidarity benefit.
    B. promotion offer.
    C. material benefit.
    D. bribe.

    C (p. 422)

17. Why is it important for interest groups to offer selective benefits?
    A. It is necessary to limit the extent of the free-rider problem.
    B. If they don't, people will join political parties instead.
    C. Selective benefits are the only way to measure the success of an interest group.
    D. All of the above.

    A (p. 422)

18. A _____ is the best example of an informational benefit provided by many interest groups.
    A. consciousness-raising workshop
    B. free T-shirt
    C. newsletter
    D. health insurance premium

    C (p. 422)

19. Approximately how many members does the AARP have?
    A. 33,000
    B. 333,000
    C. 3,300,000
    D. 33,000,000

    D (p. 423)

20. What is the primary variable for predicting the likelihood of joining an interest group?
    A. having an interest shared by others
    B. having a higher income and education
    C. already being a member of a political party
    D. having connections with government officials

    B (p. 424)

21. Interest groups most effectively serve
    A. the working classes.
    B. the powerless.
    C. the upper classes.
    D. government bureaucrats.

    C (p. 424)

22. Which of the following groups is best adapted to organizing the lower classes?
    A. a public interest group
    B. an ideological interest group
    C. a political party
    D. a business group

    C (p. 424)

23. What are political parties more capable of doing than interest groups?
    A. raising money
    B. providing solidarity benefits
    C. articulating a clear and persuasive ideology
    D. organizing people on a massive scale

    D (p. 424)

24. The increased number and importance of interest groups
    A. causes a subsequent expansion in government.
    B. is a response to an increase in the size and activity of government.
    C. is a direct result of a more broadly defined First Amendment's freedom of association.
    D. is due to the decline in the United States's multiparty system.

    B (p. 426)

25. Which of the following groups is most likely to belong to the New Politics movement?
    A. blue collar workers whose formative experience was the Great Depression
    B. veterans of World War II and the Korean War, entering college on the G.I. Bill
    C. upper-middle-class professionals, for whom the civil rights and antiwar movements of the 1960s were key experiences
    D. conservative, evangelical Southerners, reacting to the cultural changes of the 1960s

    C (p. 427)

26. Which of the following groups would be considered as part of the New Politics movement?
    A. the Christian Coalition
    B. the AFL-CIO
    C. the Sierra Club
    D. the Democratic Party

    C (p. 427)

27. The New Politics movement gave rise to what type of interest group?
    A. ideological
    B. partisan
    C. labor
    D. public interest

    D (p. 428)

28. Public interest groups differ from other types of interest groups in that
    A. they claim to serve the common good, not just their own particular interests.
    B. they were the first political associations to use the strategy of direct mailing.
    C. they were the first group to abandon lobbying and take up only grass-roots activism.
    D. unlike other interest groups, their status is like that of a charity, not a political organization.

    A (p. 428)

29. What distinguishes lobbying from other strategies of influence?
    A. Lobbying is the least expensive and the most democratic strategy of influencing government.
    B. Lobbyists try to exert pressure directly on governmental officials themselves.
    C. Lobbyist attempt to directly influence government by writing the rules themselves.
    D. Lobbying is the only form of influence that has explicit First Amendment protections from regulation.

    B (p. 428)

30. Another name for lobbying is
    A. stalking.
    B. mobilizing.
    C. petitioning.
    D. litigating.

    C (p. 428)

31. Which of the following are lobbyists NOT required by federal law to disclose?
    A. who they are working for
    B. how much they are paid
    C. who they are lobbying
    D. All of the above must be publicly disclosed.

    D (p. 428)

32. What is the most important and beneficial resource that lobbyists provide government officials?
    A. legitimacy
    B. money
    C. information
    D. campaign workers

    C (p. 428)

33. In order to have more success, many powerful lobbying groups often will hire
    A. celebrities.
    B. former members of Congress.
    C. people who are directly affected by a particular law or regulation.
    D. professors and intellectuals.

    B (p. 429)

34. Lobbying is
    A. an attempt by an individual or group to influence the passage of legislation by exerting direct pressure on members of Congress or a state legislature during floor debate.
    B. an attempt by an individual or group to influence the passage of legislation by exerting direct pressure on members of Congress or a state legislature.
    C. an attempt by an individual or group to influence the passage of legislation by exerting indirect pressure, through phone calls or e-mails, on members of Congress or a state legislature.
    D. the act of working on a reelection campaign.

    B (p. 428)

35. Approximately how many full and part-time lobbyists are in Washington, D.C.?
    A. 500
    B. 1,500
    C. 17,000
    D. 120,000

    C (p. 431)

36. What is the main difference between lobbying and gaining access?
    A. In gaining access, interest groups have a direct involvement in the decision-making process.
    B. Lobbyists have gained access when a government official becomes dependent on their particular interest group for financial support.
    C. Gaining access means that your interest group shares a former member of Congress.
    D. Gaining access is another term for bribery.

    A (pp. 431–32)

37. Which of the following best describes the most important relationship in gaining access?
    A. soft money
    B. an iron triangle
    C. free riders
    D. staff organizations

    B (p. 432)

38. Which of the following resources is most important in gaining access?
    A. money
    B. publicity
    C. time
    D. strong sponsorship

    C (p. 432)

39. A loose, informal relationship of public officials, interest groups, and activists, all concerned with the same policies, is called
    A. an iron triangle.
    B. a membership association.
    C. a New Politics movement.
    D. an issue network.

    D (p. 433)

40. An iron triangle is made up of an alliance between
    A. a legislative committee, an executive agency, and the federal courts.
    B. the federal courts, the state courts, and interest groups.
    C. a legislative committee, an interest group, and an executive agency.
    D. an interest group, an executive agency, and the media.

    C (p. 432)

41. What does it mean to capture a government agency?
    A. It means that agency officials have been bribed or otherwise illegally corrupted by an interest group.
    B. It means that former lobbyists have been appointed as government officials, in charge of running the very agencies they once lobbied.
    C. It means that a government agency is heavily influenced by an interest group that is itself being regulated by the agency.
    D. It refers to the practice of suing government agencies in order to block the implementation of regulatory codes.

    C (p. 433)

42. Which of the following is NOT a way in which an interest group can use litigation as a strategy of influence?
    A. file *amicus curiae* briefs
    B. finance lawsuits
    C. bring a suit on behalf of the group
    D. actively lobby judges

    D (p. 435)

43. When interest groups take out advertisements and hold marches, these are examples of
    A. going public.
    B. partisanship politics.
    C. lobbying.
    D. litigating.

    A (p. 436)

44. Which of the following groups has had the greatest success with a strategy of litigation?
    A. the National Chamber of Commerce
    B. the National Rifle Association
    C. the National Association for the Advancement of Colored People
    D. the Southern Christian Leadership Conference

    C (p. 435)

45. In recent years, the religious Right has had great effect on American politics through
    A. grassroots mobilization.
    B. gaining access.
    C. litigation.
    D. campaign financing.

    A (p. 437)

46. What is the primary function of a political action committee?
    A. to raise grassroots support for a particular interest
    B. to organize and coordinate a strategy of litigation
    C. to build better networks between interest groups and political parties
    D. to raise and distribute money to election campaigns

    D (p. 439)

47. Which of the following has been more heavily regulated as a result of 2002 campaign finance reforms?
    A. PACs
    B. soft money
    C. the amount a candidate may spend of his or her personal fortunes
    D. All of the above.

    B (pp. 439–40)

48. Which of the following statements about the relationship between interest groups and political parties is true?
    A. All political parties began as interest groups.
    B. It is very infrequent that interest groups try to form their own political party.
    C. There was no organizational difference between political parties and interest groups until the 1930s.
    D. Interest groups were first formed as an alternative to the corruption of party machine politics.

    B (pp. 441–42)

49. The fact that interest groups favor the wealthy and well educated can be understood as a reflection of what eternal dilemma in American politics?
    A. Liberty is often inconsistent with equality.
    B. Democracy has not been helpful in reducing the number of factions.
    C. There are no efficient means of organizing the working class in the United States.
    D. Organized associations and groups inhibit freedom.

    A (pp. 443–44)

50. Organized interest groups enhance American democracy by
    A. fielding large numbers of electable candidates.
    B. financing large numbers of election campaigns.
    C. empowering less potent segments of society.
    D. representing the interests of large numbers of people and encouraging political participation.

    D (p. 417)

140 | Chapter 11

51. The major organizational factors shared by most interest groups are
    A. very close links with the national news media; direct ties to a member of Congress; a headquarters in Washington, D.C.; and members.
    B. very close links with the national news media; connections with Hollywood; direct ties to the president of the United States; and members.
    C. leadership; money; an agency or office; and members.
    D. leadership; a rigid hierarchical structure; access to loans from the Federal Reserve; and members.

    C (p. 420)

52. The free-rider problem occurs because
    A. members of Congress are presented with many opportunities to amend a piece of legislation.
    B. the government subsidizes most forms of transportation in the United States.
    C. the benefits of a group's actions are available only to a specific segment of society.
    D. the benefits of a group's actions are broadly available and cannot be denied to nonmembers.

    D (p. 421)

53. The solidary benefits of interest groups include
    A. friendship and consciousness-raising.
    B. special services and goods.
    C. information and money.
    D. identification with the purpose or ideology of the group.

    A (p. 423)

54. One way that the American Association of Retired Persons (AARP) has been so effective at overcoming the free-rider problem is by providing _____ benefits to its members.
    A. selective
    B. solidary
    C. purposive
    D. elective

    A (p. 423)

55. Members of interest groups in the U.S. are typically people
    A. with higher levels of income and education.
    B. who work in management or professional occupations.
    C. from the lower socioeconomic levels.
    D. both A and B.

    D (p. 424)

56. Since the 1930s, the number and scale of interest groups at the national level has
    A. dramatically increased.
    B. experienced relatively modest growth.
    C. remained relatively stagnant.
    D. decreased.

    A (p. 426)

57. A grassroots lobbying campaign occurs
    A. when an interest group mobilizes its members and their families throughout the country to write their representatives in support of the group's position.
    B. when a spontaneous show of political support for a particular position manifests itself.
    C. when interest groups organize to support a dark-horse presidential candidate.
    D. before a session of Congress formally begins.

    A (p. 437)

58. After legislation is passed, interest groups often must continue their lobbying efforts
    A. with bureaucratic agencies to ensure that the legislation is fully implemented.
    B. with the U.S. Supreme Court to ensure that the legislation is judged to be constitutional.
    C. with the state legislatures to ensure that the legislation is fully implemented.
    D. the national news media to ensure that the public continues to support a policy fully.

    A (p. 433)

59. Interest groups can use the courts to influence public policy by
    A. bringing suit directly on behalf of the group.
    B. financing suits brought by individuals.
    C. filing a companion brief as *amicus curiae* to an existing court case.
    D. all of the above.

    D (p. 435)

60. A political action committees (PAC) can contribute _____ to any candidate for federal office, provided it contributes to at least five different federal candidates each year.
    A. $500
    B. $5000
    C. $50,000
    D. $500,000

    B (p. 439)

TRUE OR FALSE

1. The theory of pluralism states that all interests should be free to compete for influence and the result will be compromise and moderation.

    T (p. 416)

2. The American Bar Association is a good example of a labor group.

    F (p. 419)

3. People who benefit from the work of an interest group but who do not themselves contribute any effort or money are called free riders.

    T (p. 421)

4. Interest groups have been a successful way to politically mobilize the poor and working classes in the United States.

    F (p. 424)

5. The New Politics movement led to the proliferation of public interest groups in the 1970s.

    T (pp. 427–28)

6. Except for laws against bribery, lobbyists are shielded from any legal regulations on their activities.

    F (p. 428)

7. The iron triangle is a relationship that is established through repeated litigation of class action suits.

    F (p. 432)

8. Going public means that lobbyists register who they are, who they work for, and how much money they are paid.

    F (p. 436)

9. Historically, major interest groups do not typically form their own political parties.

    T (p. 442)

10. Alexis de Tocqueville believed that the proliferation of groups was detrimental to a democracy.

    F (p. 444)

CHAPTER 12 | Congress

MULTIPLE CHOICE

1. Which of the following is the best definition of a constituent?
   A. It is another name for a voter.
   B. It is the name for a member of Congress running for re-election.
   C. It is someone who donates money to a campaign.
   D. It is a person who lives in the district represented by a member of the legislature.

   D (p. 458)

2. Congress is a _____ legislature with _____ members.
   A. unicameral, 342
   B. bicameral, 535
   C. bicameral, 100
   D. unicameral, 630

   B (p. 458)

3. How long is the term of office for a U.S. senator?
   A. two years
   B. four years
   C. six years
   D. eight years

   C (p. 458)

4. Which of the following best describes a way in which the House differs from the Senate?
   A. The House is more centralized and organized than the Senate.
   B. The House is a looser and more deliberative body than the Senate.

C. The House's representatives are much less specialized than the Senate's members.
D. The House has a much greater level of turnover in its membership than the Senate.

A (p. 459)

5. The idea of _____ identifies the best representative as one who shares similar racial, ethnic, religious or occupational backgrounds as those she or he represents.
   A. agency representation
   B. sociological representation
   C. mirroring representation
   D. trustee representation

   B (p. 459)

6. Which idea of representation says that a legislator should be viewed as someone whom voters hire to represent their interests?
   A. agency representation
   B. sociological representation
   C. mirroring representation
   D. trustee representation

   A (p. 460)

7. As of 2003, how many women serve in the U.S. Senate?
   A. two
   B. seven
   C. thirteen
   D. twenty-one

   C (p. 460)

8. The most common occupation members of Congress had before coming to Congress was
   A. business executive.
   B. sales representative.
   C. professor.
   D. lawyer.

   D (p. 461)

9. In each House district there are approximately _____ persons.
   A. 200,000
   B. 600,000
   C. 1,200,000
   D. 2,500,000

   B (p. 463)

10. Which of the following is NOT a service often provided by representatives to their constituents?
    A. attempting to influence the decision of a regulatory commission on behalf of a constituent
    B. presenting a private bill for constituents
    C. offering constituents legal advice regarding new administrative laws
    D. writing and mailing out newsletters

    C (p. 463)

11. Constituency service is so important that
    A. representatives spend about three-quarters of their time aiding constituents.
    B. party leaders will not ask any member to vote in a way that conflicts with the interests or opinions of their district.
    C. the House and Senate have recently created a Committee on Constituency Service.
    D. All of the above.

    B (p. 463)

12. A senator or representative running for re-election is called the
    A. constituent.
    B. incumbent.
    C. elector.
    D. trustee.

    B (p. 464)

13. In recent years, approximately what percentage of House members seeking reelection successfully win their race?
    A. 60 percent
    B. 75 percent
    C. 82 percent
    D. 95 percent

    D (p. 464)

14. Which of the following best explains the low number of women in Congress?
    A. More men than women vote, and men tend not to vote for women candidates.
    B. Women do not have organizations or PACs supporting their candidacy.
    C. Incumbency is a very powerful resource, and most incumbents have been men.
    D. Women do not make very effective representatives.

    C (p. 465)

15. As the population in the United States grows and shifts, which region(s) of the country have benefited in recent redistricting?
    A. Northeast
    B. Midwest
    C. South and West
    D. A and C

    C (p. 466)

16. Redistricting is controversial because
    A. the way districts are drawn can advantage one party over another.
    B. two incumbents can be forced to run for the same seat.
    C. some states gain extra seats while other states lose seats.
    D. All of the above.

    D (p. 466)

17. What did the Supreme Court declare in *Miller v. Johnson*?
    A. Districts could not be drawn to favor the incumbent candidate.
    B. The racial composition of a district could not be the predominant factor while redistricting.
    C. Incumbents could not begin fund-raising any earlier than nine months before the general election.
    D. It was not unconstitutional for states to use a nonelected, nonpartisan committee to redistrict.

    B (p. 467)

18. The powers and resources available to government officials that are used to favor supporters are called
    A. trusteeships.
    B. expenditures.
    C. patronage.
    D. clotures.

    C (p. 467)

19. Pork-barrel legislation
    A. deals with specific projects and their location within a particular congressional district.
    B. deals with specific agricultural subsidies.
    C. funds efforts to increase the levels of America's meat exports.
    D. grants a special privilege to a person named in the bill.

    A (p. 467)

20. What are the most common private bills proposed in Congress?
    A. bills giving individuals or corporations tax relief
    B. bills for permanent visas for foreign nationals
    C. bills for defense contracts in a representative's district
    D. There are no private bills in Congress; all bills must be public.

    B (p. 468)

21. Who is the Speaker of the House?
    A. The vice president is also the Speaker of the House.
    B. The representative with the longest tenure in the House is the Speaker.
    C. The elected leader of the majority party in the House is the Speaker.
    D. An employee of Congress who formally brings the House into session each day is the Speaker.

    C (p. 470)

22. What are the origins of most of the procedures and organizations established to conduct business in Congress?
    A. the Constitution
    B. the executive branch
    C. Congress
    D. the national committees of the two major political parties

    C (p. 469)

23. In the House of Representatives, the majority leader is
    A. subordinate to the Speaker of the House.
    B. the same office as the Speaker of the House.
    C. superior in formal powers to the Speaker of the House.
    D. There is no majority leader in the House of Representatives.

    A (p. 470)

24. Who has the most formal power in the Senate?
    A. the Speaker of the Senate
    B. the majority and minority leaders
    C. the Senate pro tempore
    D. Unlike the House, all Senators are equal in power.

    B (p. 471)

25. Which of the following is NOT a task for which congressional party leaders are responsible?
    A. the organization of the House and Senate calendar
    B. the establishment of a legislative agenda

C. the assignment of members of Congress to committees when there is conflict
D. the organization of the re-election strategies of incumbents

D (p. 470)

26. The need to divide the labor of legislation is best exemplified in what formal structure of Congress?
    A. the establishment of party whips
    B. the establishment of standing committees
    C. the strict control over floor time in Congress
    D. the use of conference committees

    B (p. 472)

27. Joint committees in Congress
    A. are temporary.
    B. have officials from the executive branch on them.
    C. are composed of members from the Senate and the House.
    D. are made up of members of only one party.

    C (p. 473)

28. Organizational reforms instituted by Congress in the 1970s attempted to
    A. fragment power by reducing the power of committee chairs.
    B. centralize power into the hands of party leaders.
    C. speed up legislation by reducing the number of committees to which a bill was referred.
    D. reduce the scrutiny of the media by closing hearings to the public.

    A (p. 474)

29. Which of the following best describes the organizational changes made in Congress during the 1990s?
    A. Attempts were made to concentrate more power into the hands of party leaders.
    B. Power was decentralized by increasing the number of subcommittees.
    C. Partisan conflicts were reduced by allowing some committees to be chaired by a member of the minority party.
    D. The power of seniority was increased in the standing committees.

    A (p. 474)

30. Which of the following is NOT a task of congressional staff members?
    A. dealing with administrative agencies
    B. drafting legislative proposals
    C. organizing hearings
    D. debating and voting in subcommittee meetings

    D (pp. 474–75)

31. The Congressional Research Service and the General Accounting Office are examples of
    A. staff agencies.
    B. executive-congressional liaison offices.
    C. caucuses.
    D. select committees.

    A (p. 476)

32. Which of the following is the best definition of a congressional caucus?
    A. a formal substructure of congressional parties, oriented toward fund-raising
    B. unofficial groups of representatives or senators sharing similar interests or opinions
    C. informal lobbying groups, organized around similar interests such as agriculture or maritime affairs
    D. None of the above.

    B (p. 476)

33. Approximately what percentage of proposed bills die in committee?
    A. 40 percent
    B. 60 percent
    C. 75 percent
    D. 95 percent

    D (p. 478)

34. The determination of the time and structure of floor debate on a bill is up to the
    A. bill's authors.
    B. Rules Committee.
    C. Ways and Means Committee.
    D. majority leader.

    B (p. 478)

35. A filibuster allows members of the Senate to
    A. refer a bill to multiple committees.
    B. avoid a conference committee.
    C. prevent a vote on a bill by speaking continuously on the floor.
    D. call into question any action of the executive branch.

    C (p. 479)

36. When the House and the Senate coordinate two versions of the same bill, they often use a _____ to obtain a single unified bill.
    A. joint committee

B. conference committee
C. reconciliation committee
D. standing committee

B (pp. 479–80)

37. How can a president's veto be overridden by Congress?
    A. by a two-thirds vote by either house
    B. by a two-thirds vote by both houses
    C. by a simple majority vote by both houses
    D. A president's veto cannot be overridden.

    B (p. 480)

38. Which of the following is NOT an important influence on the legislative agenda of Congress?
    A. constituents
    B. lobbyists
    C. the president
    D. the federal courts

    D (p. 480)

39. "Astroturf lobbying" refers to the practice whereby
    A. members of Congress are influenced by being given free tickets to sporting events or other gifts.
    B. a special interest group simulating a grassroots movement works with well-organized campaigns and petitions.
    C. members of Congress are influenced by large campaign donations.
    D. lobbyists begin to specialize, with narrow areas of professional expertise.

    B (p. 483)

40. Which of the following statements about a party vote is true?
    A. A party vote is much more common now than in the nineteenth century.
    B. A party vote was disallowed by the organizational reforms of the 1970s.
    C. A party vote is more rare now than at the beginning of the twentieth century.
    D. The decline of party votes reflects the increasing strength of party discipline.

    C (p. 484)

152 | Chapter 12

41. Why does the House have greater party unity than the Senate?
    A. Representatives have more partisan constituents than senators.
    B. House leaders have more organizational control over the actions of representatives than Senate leaders do.
    C. Political parties donate more money to re-elect representatives than senators, who are more independent fund-raisers.
    D. There is, in fact, no real difference in levels of party unity between the House and Senate.

    B (p. 484)

42. Which of the following is NOT a resource congressional party leaders have at their disposal to secure the unity and cooperation of their members?
    A. committee assignments
    B. access to the floor
    C. constituency service
    D. access to leadership PACs

    C (p. 485)

43. Responsibility for communication among party members in Congress lies with the
    A. Speaker of the House and Senate pro tempore.
    B. whip system.
    C. party's national committee.
    D. party caucuses.

    B (p. 486)

44. When two members of Congress who share no common interests agree to support each other's bills, this practice is called
    A. filibustering.
    B. delegating.
    C. logrolling.
    D. bargaining.

    C (p. 490)

45. Oversight can best be described as
    A. the efforts of Congress to supervise the manner in which its laws are implemented by the executive branch.
    B. the organizational control exercised by party whips over members of Congress.
    C. the authority of committee chairs over the hearings and investigations conducted by the subcommittees.
    D. the informal power of the president to set the legislative agenda for Congress.

    A (p. 491)

46. The Senate's constitutional power of advice and consent extends to all of the following presidential powers EXCEPT
    A. the president's power to make treatises with foreign nations.
    B. the president's appointment of top executive officials, like cabinet members.
    C. the president's power to make executive agreements.
    D. all federal judges.

    C (p. 493)

47. The role the House of Representatives plays in impeachments can best be compared with that of a
    A. judge.
    B. grand jury.
    C. prosecuting attorney.
    D. defense witness.

    B (p. 494)

48. The reforms from the 1970s that opened Congress to more public scrutiny and fragmented power ultimately led to
    A. a more efficient and fair system of legislation.
    B. a reduction in the influence of partisanship.
    C. the process of lawmaking takes place with more deliberative speed.
    D. gridlock.

    D (p. 496)

49. What are the greatest dangers with a trustee model of representation?
    A. Members of Congress may not bring back enough pork-barrel projects to their district.
    B. Representatives may become inattentive to the wishes and opinions of their constituents.
    C. Members of Congress may give inadequate deference to the executive branch in the area of national security.
    D. The representatives who adopt this model are too influenced by special interest groups.

    B (p. 498)

50. The problem with the delegate model of representation is
    A. few people are well informed about all political issues.
    B. not all constituents' opinions will be heard equally.
    C. most people care about only a narrow range of issues.
    D. All of the above.

    D (p. 498)

154 | Chapter 12

51. The frequency with which they must seek reelection make members of the House
    A. more responsive to the needs of the elites in the states they represent.
    B. less responsive to the needs of the elites in the states they represent.
    C. less responsive to the needs of local interest groups in the districts they represent.
    D. more responsive to the needs of local interest groups in the districts they represent.

    D (p. 459)

52. Each member of Congress is responsible primarily to the _____ that he or she represents.
    A. chamber of Congress
    B. political party
    C. special interests
    D. constituency

    D (p. 458)

53. A number of powerful political action committees, such as _____, have emerged in the last twenty years to recruit women to run for Congress and fund their campaigns.
    A. Congressional Women's Caucus
    B. National Organization for Women
    C. National Women's Party
    D. EMILY's List

    D (p. 464)

54. Three factors related to the American electoral system affect who gets elected to office in this country, and what they do once they get there. Those factors are
    A. party affiliation, family connections, and the substance of issues raised during a campaign.
    B. who decides to run for office, incumbency, and the drawing of district lines.
    C. incumbency, franking, and party affiliation.
    D. military service, professional connections, and religious beliefs.

    B (p. 464)

55. The redistricting of congressional districts can affect the outcomes of elections by
    A. creating open seats and pitting members of the same party against each other.
    B. requiring the Supreme Court to select the winner in some congressional races.

C. allowing the state legislature to determine each party's nominees.
D. both A and B.

A (p. 466)

56. Congressional districts in each state are shaped to create an advantage for the majority party in _____, which controls the redistricting process.
    A. the U.S. House
    B. the U.S. Senate
    C. the state legislature
    D. the White House

C (p. 466)

57. Leaders of the two houses of Congress are elected every
    A. year.
    B. two years.
    C. four years.
    D. six years.

B (p. 469)

58. The most important leadership position in the U.S. House of Representatives is the
    A. president.
    B. House majority leader.
    C. House minority leader.
    D. Speaker of the House.

D (p. 470)

59. In general, members of the House seek committee assignments that will
    A. bring them the largest number of campaign donations.
    B. give them greater media exposure.
    C. allow them to influence decisions which are of special importance to voters in their districts.
    D. allow them more personal contact with the president.

C (p. 470)

60. The most important committees of Congress are the
    A. conference committees.
    B. joint committees.
    C. select committees.
    D. standing committees.

D (p. 472)

61. The jurisdiction of standing committees is
    A. related to a specific geographic region.
    B. defined by the subject matter of legislation, which often parallels the major cabinet departments or agencies.
    C. determined by the different political parties.
    D. determined by the U.S. Supreme Court.

    B (p. 472)

62. Congressional leaders form _____ committees when they want to take up an issue that falls between the jurisdiction of existing committees, to highlight an issue, or to investigate a particular problem.
    A. conference
    B. joint
    C. select
    D. standing

    C (p. 473)

63. Conference committees are
    A. permanent and involve members from both the House and the Senate but do not have the power to report legislation.
    B. temporary and are created to take up an issue that falls between the jurisdiction of existing committees, to highlight an issue, or to investigate a particular problem.
    C. permanent and have the power to write and propose legislation.
    D. temporary, involve members from both houses of Congress, and are charged with reaching a compromise on legislation once it has been passed by both the House and the Senate.

    D (p. 473)

64. The ability of a senator to speak for as long as he or she wishes so as to prevent action being taken on legislation that they oppose is called
    A. cloture.
    B. judicial review.
    C. filibustering.
    D. the rhetorical veto.

    C (p. 479)

65. Closed rule and open rule refer to congressional provisions regarding
    A. whether deliberations are closed or open to the general public.
    B. assignment to powerful committees.
    C. whether lobbyists are allowed inside Congress.
    D. floor debate on a bill.

    D (p. 478)

66. Cloture is
   A. the ability of a senator to speak for as long as he or she wishes to prevent action being taken on legislation that he or she opposes.
   B. the process by which three-fifths of the Senate can end a filibuster.
   C. the rule which allows one house of Congress to circumvent the other during the legislative process.
   D. the process by which the president can end a filibuster.

   B (p. 479)

67. A House-Senate conference report must be approved _____ before being sent to the president.
   A. by the U.S. Supreme Court
   B. by the House Rules Committee
   C. by the vice president
   D. on the floor of each house of Congress

   D (p. 480)

68. A vote on which 50 percent or more of the members of one party take one position while at least 50 percent of the members of the other party take the opposing position is called
   A. an ideological split.
   B. congressional gridlock.
   C. a party vote.
   D. a veto.

   C (p. 484)

69. In addition to pressuring members of Congress to vote a certain way on a bill, interest groups also have substantial influence in
   A. setting the legislative agenda.
   B. helping craft specific language in legislation.
   C. getting senators to filibuster debates on bills that they oppose.
   D. both A and B.

   D (p. 484)

70. The president has the power to make treaties and to appoint top executive officers, ambassadors, and federal judges, but only with the
   A. approval of the U.S. Supreme Court.
   B. concurrence of the vice president.
   C. advice and consent of the House of Representatives.
   D. advice and consent of the Senate.

   D (p. 492)

71. The two presidents to be impeached by the House of Representatives were _____ and Bill Clinton.
    A. Andrew Jackson
    B. Andrew Johnson
    C. Herbert Hoover
    D. Richard Nixon

    B (p. 494)

72. Members of Congress can represent the people in two ways: as a _____, a member of Congress acts on the express preferences of his or her constituency; as a _____, a member is more loosely tied to constituents and makes the decisions he or she thinks are best.
    A. delegate; trustee
    B. trustee; delegate
    C. representative; senator
    D. senator; representative

    A (p. 498)

TRUE OR FALSE

1. The House of Representatives has 335 members and the Senate has 100 members.

   F (p. 458)

2. By the 2000 election, the representation of women and minorities in Congress was roughly comparable to their proportions in the general population.

   F (p. 461)

3. Levels of incumbency in Congress are around 50 percent.

   F (p. 464)

4. Constituency service and private bills are common forms of patronage.
   T (p. 467)

5. The vice president also serves as Speaker of the House of Representatives and breaks tie votes.

   F (p. 470)

6. A standing committee usually has a parallel department or agency within the executive branch.

   T (p. 472)

7. A filibuster is a parliamentary device found in the Senate but not the House.

   T (p. 479)

8. Oversight is an important legislative check on the executive branch.

   T (p. 491)

9. The power of impeachment is located entirely in the Senate, as part of its advice and consent powers.

   F (p. 494)

10. Members of Congress who act on the express wishes of their constituents are called trustees.

    F (p. 498)

CHAPTER 13 | The Presidency

MULTIPLE CHOICE

1. The most common form of constitutional powers possessed by the president are _____ powers.
   A. expressed
   B. delegated
   C. implied
   D. suspected

   B (p. 510)

2. When the president infers powers from the "rights, duties and obligations" of the presidency, these are called
   A. delegated powers.
   B. necessary and proper powers.
   C. inherent powers.
   D. war powers.

   C (p. 510)

3. Which of the following attributes did the framers mean for the office of the president to possess?
   A. popularity
   B. energy
   C. extensive flexibility
   D. All of the above.

   B (p. 509)

4. Through the act of delegating powers, the national structure of government in the 1930s went from _____ to _____.
   A. constitutional, imperial

B. legislative centered, presidential centered
C. presidential centered, legislative centered
D. legally oriented, command oriented

B (p. 511)

5. What did the framers mean to accomplish by the indirect election of the president?
   A. to make a more independent and powerful chief executive
   B. to bind the president to the will of the people
   C. to make the president responsible to state and national legislatures
   D. to create an imperial presidency to counter the power of Congress

   C (p. 511)

6. The system of nominating presidential candidates, in the early 1800s, that left the candidates beholden to their party's leaders in Congress was called
   A. King Caucus.
   B. party primaries.
   C. congressional nominations.
   D. presidential gerrymandering.

   A (p. 511)

7. The rise of national conventions to nominate the president led to the empowerment of what group?
   A. Congress
   B. state party leaders
   C. the voters
   D. the candidates

   B (p. 511)

8. The president's position as head of state is defined in the Constitution by all of the following powers EXCEPT
   A. military.
   B. partisan.
   C. judicial.
   D. diplomatic.

   B (p. 512)

9. The power to declare war is given to whom under the Constitution?
   A. the president
   B. the Senate
   C. both houses of Congress
   D. the Senate with the approval of the president

   C (p. 513)

10. In undertaking the campaign against the Taliban in 2001, George W. Bush
    A. sought and received a declaration of war from Congress.
    B. sought but failed to receive a declaration of war from Congress.
    C. sought and received congressional authorization for the bombing but not a declaration of war.
    D. took action without approval from Congress.

    C (p. 513)

11. All of the following have been uses of the president's power of amnesty or pardon EXCEPT
    A. George Washington's amnesty to all Americans who fought for the British during the War for Independence.
    B. Andrew Johnson's amnesty to all Confederate soldiers.
    C. Gerald Ford's pardon of Richard Nixon for crimes he may have committed.
    D. Jimmy Carter's amnesty for all draft evaders during the Vietnam conflict.

    A (p. 515)

12. Why was George Washington's receiving Edmond Genet as ambassador of France during the French Revolution so significant?
    A. It demonstrated that the United States could use diplomacy to keep out of European conflicts.
    B. It reflects the authority of the president to officially recognize specific regimes as the official sovereign power of a nation when there is doubt as to who rules.
    C. It was the first time any nation had recognized the United States as independent.
    D. It prevented the economic embargo of American goods by the king of France.

    B (p. 515)

13. In order to get around the need for Senate approval of treaties, many contemporary presidents have made use of _____ in foreign affairs.
    A. diplomacy
    B. international protocols
    C. executive immunity
    D. executive agreements

    D (p. 515)

14. The term _____ was coined by critics who feared that the chief executive's powers had grown too great since World War II.
    A. *"Pax Americana"*
    B. "the imperial presidency"

C. "the overimmunized executive"
D. "Nixonization"

B (p. 515)

15. What was the Gulf of Tonkin Resolution?
    A. the agreement between the United States, North Korea, and South Korea, ending hostilities on the Korean peninsula
    B. congressional authorization for Lyndon Johnson to expand the American military presence in Vietnam
    C. congressional demands to cut back the number of American troops in Vietnam, after the elections of 1968
    D. the official authorization by Congress for the Gulf War of 1991

    B (p. 515)

16. The goal of the War Powers Resolution was to
    A. compel a congressional declaration of war for every large-scale military operation.
    B. check the ability of Congress to cut off funding for troops when the president sends them overseas without congressional approval.
    C. limit the power of the president to commit American troops to military action without authorization from Congress.
    D. end the Vietnam War.

    C (p. 515)

17. The president has the power to appoint all of the following, with the approval of the Senate, EXCEPT
    A. the vice president.
    B. all federal judges.
    C. cabinet secretaries.
    D. All of the above.

    A (p. 517)

18. When Dwight Eisenhower sent federal troops into Little Rock High School in 1957, it demonstrated that
    A. the president may make unilateral use of the emergency powers to protect states against domestic disorder.
    B. the president requires the federal court's approval before using troops in domestic disturbances.
    C. the use of the president's emergency powers against domestic disorder necessitates a request by the governor of the effected state.
    D. the president needs congressional authorization to use troops in domestic, as well as in international, situations.

    A (p. 520)

19. Why is the president's State of the Union address important?
    A. It is often the only time that members of Congress get to directly question the president.
    B. It is an opportunity for the president to set the legislative agenda by initiating proposals and directing public attention to the executive's goals.
    C. It is an opportunity for the president to highlight the positive actions of the previous year.
    D. It is the only time the president is constitutionally allowed to address Congress.

    B (p. 520)

20. What is required for Congress to override a presidential veto?
    A. a majority of both houses of Congress
    B. two-thirds of both houses of Congress
    C. three-fourths of both houses of Congress
    D. A president's veto cannot be overridden, unless it concerns the budget, in which case it requires a three-fourths majority of both houses.

    B (p. 521)

21. When the president strikes out only specific provisions of a bill but signs the rest, this is called a
    A. pocket veto.
    B. razor blade veto.
    C. line-item veto.
    D. prerogative veto.

    C (p. 522)

22. Which of the following does the president NOT have the constitutional power to perform?
    A. a veto
    B. a pocket veto
    C. a line-item veto
    D. The president has the power to perform all of the above.

    C (p. 522)

23. The president's power to set the debate concerning public policy in Congress is called
    A. an executive mandate.
    B. an executive privilege.
    C. a legislative initiative.
    D. an executive order.

    C (p. 522)

24. An executive order is
    A. a rule or regulation issued unilaterally by the president, with the status of a law.
    B. an emergency decree that is law only during the duration of a crisis or pending congressional approval.
    C. a demand to Congress that it vote on a particular piece of legislation.
    D. any act of the executive branch that does not have to be made public.

    A (p. 522)

25. The president's ability to make many important appointments in the executive branch is the power of
    A. prestige.
    B. a mandate.
    C. patronage.
    D. mobilization.

    C (p. 523)

26. Which of the following statements about the cabinet is INCORRECT?
    A. The cabinet has no status under the Constitution.
    B. The cabinet does not make decisions collectively.
    C. The cabinet does not meet as a group, except during the State of the Union address.
    D. The Senate must approve the president's choice of cabinet secretaries.

    C (p. 525)

27. The formal group of presidential foreign policy advisers, established in 1947, is called the
    A. State Department.
    B. National Security Council.
    C. Joint Chiefs of Staff.
    D. Council on Foreign Affairs.

    B (p. 525)

28. The groups of advisers and analysts to the president are collectively called the
    A. cabinet.
    B. kitchen cabinet.
    C. White House staff.
    D. Executive Council of Advisors.

    C (p. 526)

29. An informal group of advisers to the president is often called the
    A. kitchen cabinet.
    B. plumbers.
    C. Round Table.
    D. good ol' boys (despite the fact that many women have entered these ranks).

    A (p. 526)

30. The Office of Management and Budget and the Council of Economic Advisors are both parts of
    A. the cabinet.
    B. the White House staff.
    C. the Office of the Vice President.
    D. the Executive Office of the President.

    D (p. 527)

31. What is the primary constitutional task of the vice president, besides succeeding the president in case of death, resignation, or incapacitation?
    A. to serve as Speaker of the House of Representatives
    B. to cast tie-breaking votes in the Senate
    C. to act as chief admiral of the U.S. Navy
    D. to represent the president overseas

    B (p. 527)

32. The main political value of the vice president is to
    A. bring the president votes in the election from a group or region that would not otherwise be a likely source of support.
    B. draw negative attention away from the president during times of crisis.
    C. give the president an institutional link to Congress.
    D. act as the political party's chief fund-raiser.

    A (p. 527)

33. The First Lady is an important resource for the president in his capacity as
    A. head of government.
    B. head of state.
    C. commander in chief.
    D. legislative initiator.

    B (p. 529)

34. Presidential scholar Richard Neustadt argues that the president's greatest power is
    A. the increased military power since World War II.
    B. as head of his political party.

C. the veto.
D. the power to persuade.

D (p. 530)

35. Who was the first First Lady to seek and win public office on her own?
    A. Dolly Madison
    B. Eleanor Roosevelt
    C. Betty Ford
    D. Hillary Clinton

    D (p. 530)

36. Which of the following is NOT one of the informal political resources available to presidents?
    A. the president's political party
    B. the president's home state
    C. the election victory
    D. interest groups

    B (pp. 531–35)

37. _____ is the claim that the electorate has given the winner of a presidential election a special authority to carry out her or his plans.
    A. An inauguration
    B. Patronage
    C. A mandate
    D. An anointment

    C (p. 531)

38. When are the president's partisan ties most important?
    A. in winning support from public opinion
    B. in raising campaign funds
    C. in dealing with Congress on legislative matters
    D. in making executive appointments

    C (p. 531)

39. Which of the following groups was NOT part of the New Deal coalition?
    A. white southern conservatives
    B. Wall Street interests
    C. organized labor
    D. northern urban liberals

    B (p. 533)

168 | Chapter 13

40. Throughout the twentieth century, which group has historically been the most loyal supporter of Republican presidents?
    A. southerners
    B. organized business
    C. organized labor
    D. racial and ethnic minorities

    B (p. 531)

41. Who coined the term "bully pulpit" to describe the president's use of the media?
    A. Abraham Lincoln
    B. Theodore Roosevelt
    C. Franklin Roosevelt
    D. Ronald Reagan

    B (p. 534)

42. Franklin Roosevelt's radio broadcast fireside chats allowed him to
    A. reach over the heads of congressional opponents by appealing to their constituents directly.
    B. establish a personal relationship with the American people, through the use of personality.
    C. drum up continuing support for his programs and policies.
    D. All of the above.

    D (p. 534)

43. Which of the following statements concerning the idea of a permanent campaign is INCORRECT?
    A. It describes presidential politics in which all action is taken with re-election in mind.
    B. It allows the president to skirt many campaign finance rules and regulations.
    C. It is designed to ensure mass popularity in the polls.
    D. It ensures a continuing supply of campaign funds throughout the term in office.

    B (pp. 535–36)

44. What is the general tendency of a president's popularity?
    A. Presidents usually begin with moderate ratings which either move drastically up or down, depending on their success.
    B. Presidents usually start out popular and decline over the next four years.
    C. Presidents usually maintain the public approval ratings they had when entering office, unless there is an economic recession or international crisis.

D. No pattern has been discerned in presidential approval ratings.

B (p. 537)

45. The generally favorable reaction of the American public to actions taken by a president in foreign policy, especially during a crisis, is called the
    A. patriot leap.
    B. foreign affairs bump.
    C. rallying effect.
    D. permanent campaign.

    C (p. 537)

46. A sitting president who loses an election in November, or is not eligible for re-election, but remains in office until January is often called
    A. a lame duck.
    B. gerrymandered.
    C. mandated.
    D. imperial.

    A (p. 538)

47. Which of the following statements is a difference between parliamentary executives and presidential executives?
    A. Parliamentary executives are also members of the legislature, unlike presidents.
    B. Parliamentary executives are favored in South America, and presidential executives in North America and Europe.
    C. Presidential systems usually have less checks and balances than parliamentary systems.
    D. All of the above.

    A (p. 539)

48. Who was the first president to claim executive privilege in order not to reveal information to Congress?
    A. George Washington
    B. Abraham Lincoln
    C. Franklin Roosevelt
    D. Richard Nixon

    A (p. 528)

49. What event in American politics led to the Supreme Court restricting the use of executive privilege?
    A. the Civil War
    B. the Vietnam War
    C. the Watergate cover-up
    D. the Iran-Contra scandal

    C (p. 528)

50. The office of the presidency was established by _____ of the Constitution.
    A. Article I
    B. Article II
    C. Article III
    D. Article IV

    B (p. 510)

51. The two major roles that the American president performs are
    A. head of state and head of government.
    B. head of government and head of party.
    C. head of party and chief justice.
    D. head of state and chief justice.

    A (p. 512)

52. The president must share foreign policy powers with
    A. the Joint Chiefs of Staff.
    B. Congress.
    C. the states.
    D. the vice president.

    B (p. 513)

53. Executive agreements are different from formal treaties in that they
    A. have been ruled unconstitutional by the U.S. Supreme Court.
    B. do not have to be approved by the Senate.
    C. do not have to be approved by the House.
    D. are generally formulated at meetings of the United Nations.

    B (p. 515)

54. The _____ asserted that the president could send American troops into action abroad only in the event of a declaration of war or other statutory authorization by Congress, or if American troops were attacked or directly endangered.
    A. War Powers Act of 1973
    B. National Security Act of 1947
    C. Neutrality Act of 1937
    D. Boland Amendment of 1982

    A (p. 515)

55. The _____ is the informal designation for the heads of the major federal government departments.
    A. White House staff
    B. Committee of Staff

C. presidential advisory committee
D. cabinet

D (p. 525)

56. The claim that confidential communications deemed vital to the national interest between the president and close advisers should not be revealed without the consent of the president is called
    A. executive agreement.
    B. executive authority.
    C. executive privilege.
    D. executive order.

    C (p. 528)

57. A president who claims to possess a mandate from the American electorate could arguably
    A. claim the authority to increase taxes without the approval of Congress.
    B. ignore all legislative mandates passed by Congress.
    C. claim that voters have approved the agenda he campaigned upon, and that Congress ought therefore to approve it.
    D. claim that voters have approved the president's agenda and that the state legislatures should unhesitatingly support it.

    C (p. 531)

58. The high number of public appearances by Presidents Bill Clinton and George W. Bush is evidence of what some call
    A. the rallying effect.
    B. the permanent campaign.
    C. presidential popularity.
    D. a mandate.

    B (p. 535)

TRUE OR FALSE

1. The rise in presidential power since the New Deal is largely due to the delegation of powers from Congress.

   T (pp. 510–11)

2. The president shares his powers as commander in chief with the Senate.

   F (p. 513)

3. The War Powers Resolution was passed by Congress over the veto of Richard Nixon.

   T (p. 515)

4. The president does not have constitutional authority to use military troops domestically.

   F (p. 520)

5. The line-item veto was declared unconstitutional by the Supreme Court.

   T (p. 522)

6. The White House staff currently consists of approximately a dozen advisers and policy analysts to the president.

   F (p. 526)

7. The vice president must be confirmed by the Senate.

   F (p. 527)

8. Successful presidents have often been leaders of public opinion, rather than followers.

   T (p. 535)

9. The idea of a permanent campaign dates back to the presidency of Andrew Jackson.

   F (p. 535)

10. Public opinion is generally favorable of a president's foreign policy decisions, especially during a crisis.

    T (p. 537)

CHAPTER 14 | Bureaucracy in a Democracy

MULTIPLE CHOICE

1. "Bureaucracy," literally translated, means
   A. rule by desks.
   B. control of the anonymous.
   C. governance by experts.
   D. next window please.

   A (p. 550)

2. Who stated, in his 1996 State of the Union address, that "the era of big government is over"?
   A. George H. W. Bush
   B. Bill Clinton
   C. George W. Bush
   D. Ronald Reagan

   B (p. 550)

3. At its peak in _____, the federal bureaucracy had _____ employees, not including military personnel.
   A. 1936, 6 million
   B. 1968, 3 million
   C. 1982, 1 million
   D. 1996, 8 million

   B (p. 550)

4. Since the 1950s, the number of federal employees, compared with the entire workforce, has
   A. increased sharply.
   B. increased slightly.
   C. decreased slightly.
   D. decreased sharply.

   C (pp. 550–51)

5. The attempt of bureaucracies to translate laws into routine procedures and practices is called
   A. adjudication.
   B. regulation.
   C. deregulation.
   D. implementation.

   D (p. 553)

6. Why is communication so critical for bureaucracies?
   A. because knowledge is power
   B. because specialization separates workers whose actions must be coordinated
   C. because communication is the only way to prevent the growth of iron triangles
   D. All of the above.

   B (p. 553)

7. Which of the following has NOT been part of the aftermath of September 11?
   A. Many airline security screeners were made federal employees.
   B. The trust and respect for federal bureaucracies rose.
   C. The Office of Homeland Security was given cabinet-level status.
   D. All of the above have been part of the aftermath of September 11.

   D (pp. 547–48)

8. Which of the following statements about administrative rule making is FALSE?
   A. All federal rules must be published in the *Federal Register*.
   B. Both houses of Congress must formally approve all federal rules.
   C. All federal rules must undergo a period of public comment.
   D. All of the above statements are true.

   B (p. 554)

9. When a bureaucracy applies rules and precedents to specific cases, this is called
   A. rule making.
   B. administrative adjudication.
   C. devolution.
   D. deregulation.

   B (p. 553)

10. By the 1980s, the average length of time to develop and implement an administrative rule was
    A. two weeks.
    B. one month.
    C. thirty-five to forty months.
    D. four years.

    C (p. 554)

11. The Civil Service Act of 1883 attempted to pattern government hiring after practices found in
    A. business.
    B. the Catholic Church.
    C. Congress.
    D. local government.

    A (p. 555)

12. Before the Civil Service Act of 1883, how were government appointments handled?
    A. Appointments were made on the basis of merit.
    B. Appointments were made on the basis of seniority.
    C. Appointments were made to political supporters as part of a spoils system.
    D. The Civil Service Act of 1883 created the first federal bureaucracy.

    C (p. 555)

13. Which of the following statements about the merit system is/are NOT true?
    A. Every member of a government agency has been appointed as a part of the merit system.
    B. The merit system establishes competitive exams for jobs.
    C. The merit system gives bureaucrats job protection.
    D. All of the above.

    A (p. 555)

14. Which of the following is the most critical reason government bureaucrats are given job tenure?
    A. Job tenure is an attempt to reduce political interference in government agencies.
    B. Most tasks in government are very specialized, and it is important to retain well-trained workers.
    C. It is a way to reward and protect those with merit.
    D. Since the institution of the merit system, government workers have much less job security.

    A (p. 555)

15. The largest subunits of the federal executive branch are called
    A. agencies.
    B. units.
    C. departments.
    D. states.

    C (p. 555)

16. What is an independent agency?
    A. an agency that was not created by a law passed by Congress.
    B. an agency whose budget comes from outside funding.
    C. an agency that is not part of any cabinet department.
    D. all of the above.

    C (p. 557)

17. Which of the following is NOT an independent agency?
    A. National Aeronautics and Space Administration (NASA)
    B. Central Intelligence Agency (CIA)
    C. Federal Bureau of Investigation (FBI)
    D. Environmental Protection Agency (EPA)

    C (p. 557)

18. The head of a department is called the
    A. secretary.
    B. agency supervisor.
    C. service administrator.
    D. chief executive officer.

    A (p. 555)

19. What is the origin of most federal bureaus?
    A. Congress passes laws creating and funding most federal bureaus.
    B. The cabinet secretaries create most federal bureaus out of administrative necessity and convenience.
    C. Most federal bureaus are created by executive agreement.

D. Most federal bureaus are created by the Constitution's Article II powers.

   A (p. 555)

20. What is a government corporation?
   A. Each department in the executive branch is legally registered as a corporation.
   B. It is an agency that performs and charges for services usually provided by the private sector.
   C. It is a private company, publicly traded, whose sole investor is the federal government.
   D. It is a government agency that is charged by Congress to make a profit.

   B (p. 557)

21. Which of the following is a government corporation?
   A. the National Park Service
   B. the U.S. Postal Service
   C. the Department of Defense
   D. the Federal Bureau of Investigation

   B (p. 557)

22. The first regulatory agencies established by Congress were
   A. in the Department of Commerce.
   B. independent agencies.
   C. government corporations.
   D. in the Labor Department.

   B (p. 557)

23. Which of the following is NOT a department responsible for promoting the public welfare?
   A. the Department of Health and Human Services
   B. the Department of State
   C. the Department of the Interior
   D. the Department of Veterans Affairs

   B (p. 558)

24. The National Park Service is located in
   A. the Department of the Interior.
   B. the Department of Agriculture.
   C. the Department of Energy.
   D. It is an independent agency.

   A (p. 560)

25. A bureau charged with putting restrictions and obligations on individuals or corporations in the private sector is called a _____ agency.
    A. redistributive
    B. police
    C. regulatory
    D. fiscal

    C (p. 560)

26. Ronald Reagan's inability to dismantle the Department of Education reflects the power of
    A. the merit system.
    B. iron triangles.
    C. the *Federal Registry*.
    D. devolution.

    B (pp. 561–62)

27. Which of the following is the best description of an iron triangle?
    A. the stable relationship between a bureaucratic agency, a clientele group, and a legislative committee
    B. the inability to reform federal rules without help from the House of Representatives, the Senate, and the president
    C. the domination of a few large companies in the regulation of iron mining and smelting
    D. the breakdown in the separation of powers between the Congress, the federal judiciary, and the president

    A (p. 561)

28. The response to the Department of Agriculture's attempt to classify ketchup as a vegetable in school lunches reveals
    A. cost-cutting measures often fail to pass Congress.
    B. bureaucratic agencies, like politicians, must pay attention to public opinion.
    C. the great influence of the condiment industry.
    D. the intractable power of the iron triangle.

    B (p. 562)

29. Which of the following is NOT a federal department entrusted with providing national security?
    A. Defense
    B. State
    C. Police
    D. Justice

    C (p. 562)

30. The USA PATRIOT Act
    A. stated Congress's approval of the invasion of Afghanistan.
    B. allows the attorney general to detain any foreigner suspected of posing a threat to internal security.
    C. grants authority over immigration cases to the Defense Department.
    D. gave the Justice Department jurisdiction over all prisoners taken in Afghanistan.

    B (p. 564)

31. Which of the following has not been part of the history of the FBI?
    A. interrogating suspects in Afghanistan
    B. monitoring the KKK and other hate groups
    C. filing lawsuits against the Mafia
    D. infiltrating the civil rights movement

    C (pp. 564–65)

32. How are ambassadors chosen?
    A. They are part of the federal bureaucracy's merit system.
    B. They are selected by the president, often as patronage for large campaign donations.
    C. They are selected by the Secretary of State.
    D. They are elected to four years terms of office, by the nation to whom they will be ambassador.

    B (pp. 565, 568)

33. Which of the following is NOT part of the Justice Department?
    A. the Civil Rights Division
    B. the Immigration and Naturalization Service
    C. the Internal Revenue Service
    D. the Federal Bureau of Investigation

    C (pp. 564–65)

34. _____ is the primary mission of the State Department.
    A. Military protection
    B. Diplomacy
    C. International aid
    D. Transnational commerce

    B (p. 565)

35. The Freedom of Information Act is designed to
    A. lead to quicker filing of *habeas corpus* petitions.
    B. make more national security documents available to the public.
    C. prevent inefficiency and waste in government management.
    D. expand the freedom of speech granted to government employees.

    B (p. 572)

36. The use of taxing and spending powers to shape the economy is part of _____ policy.
    A. fiscal
    B. monetary
    C. regulatory
    D. distributive

    A (p. 573)

37. Who has authority to set interest rates and lending activities for the nation's banks?
    A. the Federal Reserve Board
    B. the Secretary of the Treasury
    C. the Internal Revenue Service
    D. the Securities and Exchange Commission

    A (p. 574)

38. Which of the following is a good example of a revenue agency?
    A. the Federal Reserve System
    B. the Agricultural Extension Service
    C. the U.S. Custom Service
    D. All of the above.

    C (p. 574)

39. Which of the following is NOT a clientele agency?
    A. the Internal Revenue Service
    B. the Department of Veterans Affairs
    C. the Department of Education
    D. the Social Security Administration

    A (p. 560–62, 574)

40. According to the text, what would be the most likely outcome if the federal government were to cease all economic regulation?
    A. The marketplace would work more efficiently and quickly.
    B. The marketplace would favor the more numerous workers, rather than the corporate interests.
    C. The marketplace would fall into chaos.
    D. The marketplace would more quickly globalize.

    C (p. 575)

41. What was the mission of the National Performance Review?
    A. to reorganize the federal bureaucracy to make it more efficient, accountable, and less wasteful
    B. to review each administrative agency every four years to determine whether it is necessary

C. to analyze the job performance of federal employees
D. to make recommendations to Congress on government reforms

A (p. 576)

42. What is the principle job of the Office of Homeland Security?
    A. to investigate and root out terrorist cells in the United States
    B. to coordinate the communication and activities of about fifty federal agencies that are involved in domestic security
    C. to establish a domestic version of the CIA
    D. to organize and facilitate the detention of overseas prisoners of war

    B (p. 566)

43. Which of the following is a problem with instituting administrative reform?
    A. No reform package will last past the administration of the president who proposes it.
    B. Powerful constituencies attempt to block changes they believe will harm their interests.
    C. Agencies are anxious to protect their own jurisdiction and budgets.
    D. All of the above.

    D (pp. 576–77)

44. During the administrations of Ronald Reagan and George H. W. Bush, how many federal agencies or programs were terminated?
    A. 0
    B. 10
    C. 26
    D. 137

    A (p. 579)

45. Which of the following is the best definition of deregulation?
    A. reducing the number of regulatory agencies in the federal bureaucracy
    B. giving regulatory tasks to state and local governments
    C. shrinking the number of government restraints on the conduct of private persons and corporations
    D. All of the above are forms of deregulation.

    C (p. 579)

46. When the federal government passes down to state or local government the authority to administer a program, this is called
    A. deregulation.
    B. devolution.
    C. termination.
    D. privatization.

    B (p. 579)

47. Which of the following statements is the definition of privatization?
    A. a way to shrink the federal budget by selling government services or property in the private sector
    B. a way to reduce government costs by relocating government programs to private groups or corporations
    C. a way to reduce big government by doing without some of the programs it once provided
    D. All of the above are definitions of privatization.

    B (p. 580)

48. Which of the following presidents was most concerned with managing and reorganizing the executive bureaucracy?
    A. Richard Nixon
    B. Jimmy Carter
    C. Ronald Reagan
    D. Bill Clinton

    B (p. 583)

49. Which of the following is the most constitutionally essential way to make the bureaucracy responsible?
    A. more efficient executive management
    B. further devolution
    C. congressional oversight
    D. more administrative courts

    C (p. 585)

50. Which of the following is NOT a way in which Congress can exercise oversight?
    A. individual constituency case work
    B. committee hearings and investigations
    C. budgeting process
    D. All of the above are forms of oversight.

    D (pp. 585–86)

51. The Civil Service Act of 1883 required that
    A. all government bureaucrats be personally nominated by the president.
    B. holders of a public office be qualified for the job to which they were appointed.
    C. holders of a public office possess at least a bachelor's degree from an accredited college or university.
    D. all government bureaucrats be members of the American Independent Party.

    B (p. 555)

52. Devolution describes a process by which
    A. Congress gives up some of its power to the executive branch.
    B. the federal government is downsized by delegating the implementation of programs to state and local governments.
    C. state and local governments are downsized by delegating the implementation of programs to the federal government.
    D. the U.S. delegates some of its power to the U.N.

    B (p. 579)

53. One drawback of devolution is that
    A. the standards associated with particular programs become increasingly rigid and hard to enforce.
    B. the standards associated with particular programs become increasingly variable.
    C. Congress is removed completely from the U.S.'s foreign policy process.
    D. programs become much more difficult to budget.

    B (p. 580)

54. The concept of oversight refers to the effort made by
    A. Congress to make executive agencies accountable for their actions.
    B. the president to make Congress accountable for its actions.
    C. the courts to make the legislative and executive branches responsible for their actions.
    D. the states to make the federal government responsible for its actions.

    A (p. 585)

55. The most visible indication of oversight is the
    A. use of a unanimous Supreme Court opinion by the lower federal courts to generate public support for a particular policy.
    B. use of the nullification power by the states to declare an act of the federal government unconstitutional.
    C. use of public hearings before congressional committees and subcommittees.
    D. budget deficit.

    C (p. 586)

56. Individual members of Congress can discover questions of public responsibility when engaged in
    A. a filibuster.
    B. constituent case work.
    C. activities related to the work of a conference committee.
    D. a party caucus.

    B (p. 586)

TRUE OR FALSE

1. Government bureaucracies have lawmaking responsibilities.

   T (p. 553)

2. Cabinet secretaries and undersecretaries are chosen through the merit system.

   F (p. 555)

3. Amtrak is a good example of a government corporation.

   T (p. 557)

4. Since the 1970s, the federal government has established no new regulatory programs.

   T (p. 557)

5. Iron triangles disappeared as a result of the Civil Service Act of 1883.

   F (p. 561)

6. The Federal Bureau of Investigation is located in the Office of Homeland Security.

   F (p. 564)

7. The Reagan administration terminated several government agencies during the 1980s.

   F (p. 579)

8. Devolution may lead to disparities in service throughout the different states.

   T (p. 580)

9. Bureaucracies must be rendered accountable by the president and Congress.

   T (p. 581)

10. The power of the purse is the greatest tool of oversight belonging to the president.

    F (p. 586)

CHAPTER 15 | The Federal Courts

MULTIPLE CHOICE

1. The size of the U.S. Supreme Court is set by
   A. the U.S. Constitution.
   B. Congress.
   C. a national convention.
   D. the American Bar Association.

   B (p. 599)

2. Which branch of the new government did the framers call the "least dangerous branch"?
   A. the Senate
   B. the Supreme Court
   C. the system of state courts
   D. the president

   B (p. 594)

3. Which of the following is the essence of the rule of law?
   A. Every state needs to have a written constitution.
   B. Every state must have an established system of common law.
   C. Every state needs to make its laws public.
   D. Every state must judge government officials by the same laws as its citizens are judged.

   D (p. 595)

4. In what type of law is the government always the plaintiff?
   A. public law
   B. criminal law
   C. civil law
   D. common law

   B (p. 595)

5. If a private individual brought a suit against a corporation for breaking a contract, this lawsuit would involve what kind of law?
   A. criminal
   D. civil
   C. public
   D. plaintiff

   B (p. 595)

6. The party that brings a complaint in court is called the _____, and the one against whom the complaint is brought is called the _____.
   A. defendant, plaintiff
   B. plaintiff, precedent
   C. plaintiff, defendant
   D. litigator, juror

   C (p. 595)

7. The doctrine of _____ requires courts to follow authoritative prior decisions when ruling on a case.
   A. *stare decisis*
   B. *habeas corpus*
   C. *lex talions*
   D. *ex post facto*

   A (p. 596)

8. Which of the following scenarios would most likely lead to a trial involving public law?
   A. a suspect has been caught robbing a store
   B. a passerby trips on a rake left in someone's front yard and chips a tooth
   C. a citizen accuses the police of searching her house without a warrant
   D. a doctor is accused of malpractice

   C (p. 596)

9. Approximately what percentage of all court cases in the United States are heard in federal courts?
   A. 1 percent

B. 10 percent
C. 30 percent
D. 55 percent

A (p. 596)

10. When a case is resolved through a negotiated agreement before a full trial is completed, this is called
    A. a misdemeanor.
    B. a plea bargain.
    C. taking the Fifth.
    D. a writ of *certiorari*.

    B (p. 596)

11. What is the Uniform Commercial Code?
    A. a federal law establishing common practices in each state regarding commercial affairs
    B. a set of codes states may voluntarily adopt, in order to reduce interstate differences in judicial opinions
    C. judicial guidelines established by the Supreme Court explaining the meaning of federal economic regulations
    D. a federal law regulating all forms of advertisements throughout the United States

    B (p. 597)

12. The area of authority possessed by a court, in terms of either subject area or geography, is called its
    A. appellate scope.
    B. judicial review.
    C. precedents.
    D. jurisdiction.

    D (p. 597)

13. The right of due process is best described as the right of
    A. everyone to appeal their trial.
    B. every citizen to vote.
    C. every person not to be treated arbitrarily by a government official or agency.
    D. every person to be a lawyer.

    C (p. 598)

14. Each year, the Supreme Court receives about _____ appeals and hears about _____ of them in full court.
    A. 1,000, 500
    B. 200, 10
    C. 7,500, 85
    D. 12,000, 300

    C (p. 598)

15. In which of the following types of cases does the Supreme Court have original jurisdiction?
    A. in any case involving the Constitution
    B. in any case involving an ambassador
    C. in any case involving the president
    D. All of the above.

    B (p. 598)

16. Trial courts in the federal judicial system are called
    A. grand juries.
    B. district courts.
    C. appellate courts.
    D. administrative courts.

    B (p. 598)

17. Which of the following statements about the U.S. Courts of Appeals is INCORRECT?
    A. The appeals courts were created by Congress, not by the Constitution.
    B. The appeals courts are able to hear all cases involving federal law, but not constitutional law.
    C. About 10 percent of federal cases are heard by the appeals courts.
    D. There are over ten appeals courts in the United States.

    B (p. 599)

18. What is the main function of the chief justice of the Supreme Court?
    A. The chief justice decides what cases will be heard by the full Court each term.
    B. The chief justice always writes the Court's majority opinions.
    C. The chief justice presides over the Court's public sessions and private conferences.
    D. The chief justice is also the constitutional adviser to the president.

    C (p. 599)

19. How many justices currently serve on the Supreme Court?
    A. seven
    B. nine

C. eleven
D. fifteen

B (p. 599)

20. What was known as the court-packing plan?
    A. the decision in the early nineteenth century that all federal courts should be guarded by members of the armed forces
    B. the attempt by the Republican dominated Senate of the 1990s to confirm as many conservative judges as possible
    C. the attempt by Franklin D. Roosevelt to add sympathetic justices to the Supreme Court in order to get New Deal laws upheld as constitutional
    D. the desire in Congress during the 1890s to expand the number of federal courts, to ease the workload of the Supreme Court

    C (p. 600)

21. When appointing federal judges, senatorial courtesy requires that
    A. the president will not appoint judges who do not receive the support of their home state senators.
    B. each of the president's judicial nominees must be confirmed by a majority of the Senate.
    C. the Senate Judiciary Committee will be allowed to indicate to the president which judges they won't confirm before nominations are offered.
    D. the Senate will be formally informed by the president of who has been appointed to the federal bench.

    A (p. 600)

22. The Senate must confirm
    A. only Supreme Court and U.S. Court of Appeals nominations.
    B. only Supreme Court nominations.
    C. all federal judicial nominations.
    D. all federal and most state judicial nominations.

    C (p. 600)

23. Which of the following is NOT true regarding the process of confirming judicial appointments?
    A. The full Senate will not vote on a nominee if the nominee is rejected by the Senate Judiciary Committee.
    B. The Senate must approve a nominee by a two-thirds vote.
    C. Over the past decade, the confirmation process has become politicized, as candidates are accused of being too liberal or conservative.
    D. Interest groups have recently become involved in lobbying during the confirmation process.

    B (pp. 600–601)

24. Through the exercise of _____, the Supreme Court has held actions or laws of the executive and legislative branches unconstitutional.
    A. *stare decisis*
    B. writs of *certiorari*
    C. judicial review
    D. clemency

    C (p. 604)

25. Why is the Supreme Court case of *Marbury v. Madison* important?
    A. In this case, the Court declared the authority of Congress to regulate the economy of the United States.
    B. In this case, the Court nationalized the Bill of Rights.
    C. In this case, the Court authorized itself to declare laws passed by Congress unconstitutional.
    D. In this case, the Court declared the succession of the Confederate states in violation of the Constitution.

    C (p. 605)

26. In what year was *Marbury v. Madison* decided?
    A. 1789
    B. 1803
    C. 1861
    D. 1929

    B (p. 605)

27. The power of the Supreme Court to review state actions and legislation comes from
    A. the judicial review clause of Article III.
    B. the supremacy clause of Article VI.
    C. the Tenth Amendment.
    D. *Marbury v. Madison*.

    B (p. 605)

28. Which of the following was NOT a case involving the Supreme Court's overturning a state law?
    A. *Marbury v. Madison*
    B. *Brown v. Board of Education*
    C. *Griswold v. Connecticut*
    D. *Loving v. Virginia*

    A (p. 605)

29. What is common law?
    A. another name for federal law
    B. law made by judges through their decisions which become precedents

C. law made by an administrative body
D. law that are guided by the Constitution

B (p. 607)

30. When Oliver Wendell Holmes said that lawyers make "prophecies of what courts will do in fact," he meant
    A. judges' rulings have the force of law.
    B. judges are arbitrary and there is no telling what they will decide.
    C. the law is carefully defined by the legislature for the judge to deductively apply.
    D. a lawyer is no better than a fortune-teller.

    A (p. 607)

31. Which of the following is NOT part of the *Miranda* rule?
    A. Arrested people have a right to remain silent.
    B. Arrested people have the right to know that anything they say will be used against them.
    C. Arrested people have a right to a lawyer present during interrogations.
    D. All of the above are part of the *Miranda* rule.

    D (p. 609)

32. The requirement of standing means that parties in a case must
    A. be alive.
    B. have a concrete injury or interest at stake.
    C. be present in court during the trial.
    D. know the law they are using to defend themselves.

    B (p. 610)

33. The case *Baker v. Carr* concerns
    A. desegregation of schools.
    B. redistricting.
    C. unwarranted searches and seizures.
    D. the separation of church and state.

    B (p. 609)

34. In *Roe v. Wade*, the Supreme Court was required to rule on the issue of _____, due to the fact that the pregnancy had already come to term.
    A. jurisdiction
    B. standing
    C. ripeness
    D. mootness

    D (p. 610)

35. Cases between two or more states are originally heard by
    A. both state supreme courts simultaneously.
    B. the federal district court in the state that initiates the lawsuit.
    C. the federal circuit court of appeals.
    D. the Supreme Court.

    D (p. 610)

36. A writ of *certiorari* is granted when
    A. the Constitution requires the Supreme Court to hear a case.
    B. at least four justices of the Court agree to hear a case.
    C. there is an issue that involves an interpretation of the Constitution.
    D. All of the above.

    B (p. 611)

37. Most cases reach the Supreme Court through the
    A. writ of appeal.
    B. writ of *certiorari*.
    C. writ of *habeas corpus*.
    D. writ of *amicus curiae*.

    B (p. 611)

38. Prisoners who are challenging their conviction are most likely to file a writ of
    A. *habeas corpus*.
    B. *certiorari*.
    C. jurisdiction.
    D. *stare decisis*.

    A (p. 611)

39. Which of the following best describes the role of the solicitor general?
    A. the chief legal council for the White House
    B. the lawyer who represents the United States before the Supreme Court in cases where the federal government is a party
    C. the chief lawyer for Congress who makes advisory opinions on the constitutionality of legislative proposals
    D. the head of the Department of Justice

    B (p. 612)

40. A person, agency, or interest group not directly a party to a case but with an interest in its outcome may file a(n) _____ brief.
    A. *certiorari*
    B. *per curiam*
    C. *amicus curiae*
    D. standing

    C (p. 613)

41. When the Supreme Court refuses to review a lower-court decision, announcing this decision through a brief unsigned opinion, it is called _____ opinion.
    A. a *per curiam*
    B. an *ex parte*
    C. a concurrence
    D. an *amicus curiae*

    A (p. 613)

42. Aside from the justices themselves, who or what has the greatest power in shaping the flow of cases to the Supreme Court?
    A. the attorney general
    B. the solicitor general
    C. the Senate judiciary committee
    D. the state supreme courts

    B (p. 613)

43. When interest groups involved in litigation pursue what is called a pattern of cases, this means that they are
    A. using legal arguments that have won in the past.
    B. bringing the same type of suit into multiple circuits, hoping that a contradiction in rulings will bring about a Supreme Court review.
    C. shopping around for the district where the likelihood of a favorable decision is highest.
    D. filing multiple friend of the court briefs, in the hope of influencing the legal arguments of the Supreme Court.

    B (pp. 614–15)

44. When justices agree with the ruling of a court majority but not all of its reasoning, they may often write a(n)
    A. dissent.
    B. concurrence.
    C. *ex parte*.
    D. *per curiam*.

    B (p. 617)

45. What is the significance of dissenting opinions?
    A. They are made to appeal to a justice's constituency groups.
    B. They have as much weight as law as the majority's opinion does.
    C. Dissents are signs that the Court is in disagreement on an issue and could change its ruling.
    D. Dissents are meant to confuse lawyers and government officials as to the true meaning of a decided case.

    C (p. 619)

46. If someone is an advocate of judicial restraint, he or she believes
    A. in looking only at the words of the Constitution in order to understand its meaning.
    B. that the Court should beware of overturning the judgments of popularly elected legislatures.
    C. that judges should limit their interpretations to the intention of the law's framers.
    D. All of the above.

    D (p. 620)

47. What percentage of Bill Clinton's nominees to the federal courts were women?
    A. 10 percent
    B. 33 percent
    C. 45 percent
    D. 60 percent

    B (p. 624)

48. Andrew Jackson reputedly said, "John Marshall has made his decision, now let him enforce it." What did he mean by this statement?
    A. The federal courts depend on Congress to fund the judicial police force.
    B. The Supreme Court is unable to enforce its decisions without the aid of the executive branch.
    C. It was time for Marshall to become an attorney general.
    D. Jackson wasn't going to let Marshall serve him a subpoena.

    B (p. 625)

49. Which of the following is NOT a traditional limitation on the power of the federal courts?
    A. strict rules of standing
    B. the ability of Congress to reduce federal judges' salaries
    C. the inability of the court to offer relief to classes of people
    D. the inability to enforce their own decisions

    B (p. 625)

50. A single lawsuit involving thousands of smokers suing a tobacco company would be a good example of
    A. a class action suit.
    B. a plea bargain.
    C. public law.
    D. *amicus curiae.*

    A (p. 628)

51. In recent years, federal court appointments have
    A. been characterized by strict neutrality on the part of Congress.
    B. attracted very little attention from the media and special interest groups.
    C. been characterized by intense partisan and ideological efforts to support or defeat the candidate.
    D. been unaffected by ideological concerns.

    C (p. 603)

52. Activist judges believe that the courts should
    A. always overrule state legislatures and governors when making decisions.
    B. interpret the U.S. Constitution according to the intentions of its framers and to defer to the views of Congress when interpreting federal statutes.
    C. be more aggressive and ideological than the president when vacancies occur on the court.
    D. go beyond the words of a Constitution or a statute to consider the broader societal implications of its decisions.

    D (p. 620)

53. Since the early 1990s, the Supreme Court has adopted a more _____ position on civil rights, affirmative action, abortion rights, criminal procedures, voting rights, desegregation, and the power of the national government.
    A. liberal
    B. conservative
    C. libertarian
    D. populist

    B (p. 620)

TRUE OR FALSE

1. The doctrine of *stare decisis* compels judges to use precedents to decide cases.

   T (p. 596)

2. Since the New Deal, the majority of litigation in the United States is found in federal courts.

   F (p. 596)

3. Thirty percent of lower federal court cases are accepted for review by the courts of appeals.

   F (p. 599)

4. The process of judicial confirmations is a low-key and uncontroversial affair.

   F (p. 604)

5. Judicial review over acts of Congress was established by *Marbury v. Madison*.

   T (p. 605)

6. The Supreme Court does not offer advisory opinions to any government agency concerning the probable constitutionality of a law or action.

   T (p. 610)

7. The Supreme Court has no discretion over the cases it hears each term.

   F (p. 610)

8. Only a government organization is permitted to file *amicus curiae* briefs in a case involving the constitution.

   F (p. 613)

9. Earl Warren and William O. Douglas are known as judicial activists.

   T (p. 620)

10. The role of the judiciary has gotten narrower and weaker since World War II.

    F (p. 628)

CHAPTER 16 | Government and the Economy

MULTIPLE CHOICE

1. Which of the following was NOT a reason for Congress to enact a $15 billion financial aid package for the airline industry after September 11?
   A. It was necessary to promote the public welfare and safety.
   B. The airline industry is essential to a healthy economy.
   C. The government desired to promote and regulate competition among airlines.
   D. The airlines are partially owned by the federal government, and Congress was protecting its investment.

   D (pp. 637–38)

2. When the government's goals are embodied in a law or an order, backed by punishments or rewards, this is best described as a
   A. public policy.
   B. regulation.
   C. administrative rule making.
   D. legislation.

   A (p. 639)

3. Public policy can be embodied in all of the following forms EXCEPT
   A. a law.
   B. an administrative rule.
   C. an edict.
   D. All of the above are forms of public policy.

   D (p. 639)

4. Which of the following statements about the relationship between government and capitalism is FALSE?
   A. Government makes it possible for markets to function efficiently.
   B. Government rule making means that people no longer need to rely on personal trust when conducting business.
   C. Before the Progressive Era, the marketplace had been untouched by government interference.
   D. Markets break down in nations that have a weak government.

   C (p. 639)

5. Which of the following is the best description of the changing expectations of government's role in the economy since the 1930s?
   A. People hold the government responsible for a healthy economy.
   B. People demand that the government provide Social Security and unemployment insurance.
   C. People expect that the government will engage in deficit spending for the public welfare.
   D. People expect the government to print more money in times of inflation.

   A (p. 640)

6. The rise of Napster and other music exchange services demonstrates
   A. that the federal government does not extend copyright protection to music.
   B. that new technologies have made it more difficult for the government to protect property.
   C. that the Internet is not considered to be part of the marketplace.
   D. All of the above.

   B (p. 641)

7. Why do many businesses prefer Congress to regulate the economy?
   A. Regulations are more cost effective in the long run.
   B. One national regulation is better than the inconsistencies and disparities of different state laws.
   C. Businesses argue that regulations help to increase their market share.
   D. It leads to a fairer and more equitable marketplace.

   B (p. 642)

8. Which of the following is the best example of a public good?
   A. a computer
   B. the interstate highway system

C. the airline industry
D. the Statue of Liberty

B (p. 644)

9. Who first elaborated the theory of a laissez-faire economy?
   A. John Locke
   B. Adam Smith
   C. John Maynard Keynes
   D. Milton Friedman

B (p. 645)

10. Classic laissez-faire theory argues all of the following EXCEPT
    A. government monopolies depressed economic growth.
    B. people's selfishness could promote the public good.
    C. a truly efficient government allows private enterprise to provide for all government services.
    D. economic competition unleashes growth and innovation.

C (p. 645)

11. Which of the following is the most important economic value for supporters of laissez-faire?
    A. equality
    B. efficiency
    C. fairness
    D. control

B (p. 645)

12. The idea that government intervention will fail because people will expect and compensate for such actions is called
    A. the invisible hand.
    B. the theory of rational expectations.
    C. the prisoner's dilemma.
    D. the fetishism of commodities.

B (p. 645)

13. The idea that the government can stimulate a slow economy by increasing public spending or cutting taxes is called
    A. laissez-fair economics.
    B. Keynesianism.
    C. social democracy.
    D. rational choice theory.

B (p. 646)

14. Which of the following is the key argument of John Maynard Keynes?
   A. When businesses lay off workers, those workers spend less money, forcing more layoffs.
   B. Government regulations during economic depressions must be lifted, because they destroy the already slim profit margin.
   C. The economy of size shows that monopolies are the most efficient way to distribute goods throughout a national marketplace.
   D. A well-functioning economy need never experience an economic downturn.

   A (p. 646)

15. Which U.S. president formerly said, "I am now a Keynesian"?
   A. Herbert Hoover
   B. Richard Nixon
   C. Ronald Reagan
   D. George W. Bush

   B (p. 646)

16. What economic development, according to many critics, has made Keynesian economics less useful?
   A. the end of the cold war
   B. the rise of international trade
   C. the Internet
   D. the rise of a service economy

   B (p. 646)

17. Those who believe in _____ argue that the government's role in regulating the economy should be limited to regulating the supply of money.
   A. Keynsianism
   B. monetarism
   C. fiscalism
   D. inflation

   B (p. 646)

18. Which of the following best describes the views of the economist Milton Friedman?
   A. Government is obligated to increase spending when private businesses are unable to stimulate growth.
   B. Government involvement in the economy is a restriction of individual liberty.
   C. Capitalism promotes inequality that in time will harm the foundations of democratic governance.

D. The government should enact high tariffs to make non-American goods too expensive to be competitive with American products.

B (p. 646)

19. Which of the following has NOT been a major goal of the government's involvement in the economy?
    A. promoting economic equity and fairness for all citizens
    B. promoting economic stability
    C. encouraging business development and innovation
    D. regulating international trade

    A (p. 647)

20. What event marked the major historical turning point in the relationship between the government and the marketplace?
    A. the Civil War
    B. the Depression of 1896
    C. the Great Depression
    D. World War II

    C (p. 647)

21. The index of the total output of goods and services produced in a national economy is called the
    A. federal fund rates.
    B. inflation index.
    C. gross domestic product.
    D. monetary fund.

    C (p. 648)

22. Which of the following is NOT one of the three basic prerequisites for economic growth?
    A. strong investment
    B. productive workforce
    C. technological innovation
    D. well-compensated corporate leaders

    D (p. 649)

23. What is the most important way in which the government effects personal and corporate investments?
    A. granting tax breaks for stock gains and losses
    B. promoting investor confidence through policies enforcing stability and regard for the law
    C. allowing Social Security pensions to be invested in the stock market
    D. requiring that all stock and bond transfers remain confidential

    B (p. 649)

24. Which of the following is NOT a function of the Securities and Exchange Commission?
    A. It requires companies to disclose information about the stocks and bonds that they are selling.
    B. It informs buyers of investment risks.
    C. It protects the confidentiality of all sales of stocks and bonds.
    D. It protects investors against frauds.

    C (p. 649)

25. What did the Great Depression and World War II do to the public's expectations regarding employment?
    A. They made Americans realize that unemployment was an unfortunate but largely unremediable occurrence.
    B. They made Americans realize that unemployment could only be solved by a major international crisis, like a war.
    C. They showed that the government could help to ensure full employment.
    D. They showed that the government could only solve unemployment when inflation levels were kept high.

    C (p. 650)

26. When the price level of goods and services increases over several months, this is called
    A. monetarism.
    B. a deficit.
    C. open market operations.
    D. inflation.

    D (p. 650)

27. All of the following are strategies to combat inflation EXCEPT
    A. pushing up interest rates, in order to restrain the amount of credit in the economy.
    B. increasing the amount of government spending on public works projects.
    C. instituting wage and price controls.
    D. cutting taxes.

    B (p. 651)

28. Which of the following is a way in which the government promotes business development?
    A. subsidies
    B. tax breaks

C. loans
D. All of the above.

D (p. 652)

29. Promoting and advertising American goods and services in foreign nations is one of the major tasks of
    A. the State Department.
    B. the Defense Department.
    C. the Commerce Department.
    D. the Treasury Department.

    C (p. 653)

30. What does it mean for a nation to be granted most favored nation status?
    A. It means that the United States offers that nation the lowest tariff rate offered to any other nation.
    B. It means that the United States agrees to invest in that nation, and vice versa.
    C. It means that that nation is allowed to trade with the United States without any tariff.
    D. It means that the United States has allowed that nation into the World Trade Organization.

    A (p. 653)

31. The goal of NAFTA is to
    A. grant most favored nation status to Canada and Mexico.
    B. reduce and eliminate tariffs between the United States, Canada, and Mexico.
    C. unify the North American economy around the U.S. dollar, in order to compete with the European Union.
    D. offer Canadian and Mexican workers more access to the American labor market.

    B (p. 653)

32. What organization, founded in 1995, is designed to promote international free trade?
    A. the U.N. Free Trade Fund
    B. the World Trade Organization
    C. the North American Free Trade Agreement
    D. the World Monetary Fund

    B (p. 653)

33. Before the 1930s, relations between labor and management in the United States were
    A. defined by peaceful negotiations.
    B. heavily regulated by the national government.
    C. among the most violent in the world.
    D. dependent on labor unions for stability.

    C (p. 655)

34. Most of the groundbreaking environmental laws were written in the
    A. 1960s.
    B. 1970s.
    C. 1980s.
    D. 1990s.

    B (pp. 656–57)

35. Upton Sinclair's 1906 expose, *The Jungle,* revealed
    A. the widespread use of child labor in coal mines and factories throughout the United States.
    B. the violent suppression of labor unions by big business.
    C. the control of politicians by corporate interests who run the political machines.
    D. the unsanitary practices at meatpacking plants.

    D (p. 657)

36. Which of the following statements about the Federal Reserve Board (FRB) is FALSE?
    A. The FRB is part of the Department of the Treasury.
    B. The FRB is the main organization for setting monetary policy.
    C. The members of the FRB are selected by the president and confirmed by the Senate.
    D. The president cannot remove at will the members of the FRB.

    A (p. 660)

37. What is the reserve requirement?
    A. the requirement that the federal government have at least 10 percent of the federal deficit on hand in liquid assets at all times
    B. the rule that every bank must have a certain amount of cash and negotiable securities on hand at all times
    C. the demand that there should never be more money circulating in print or computer accounts than there is gold in the U.S. Bank
    D. the requirement that the Federal Reserve Board limit the deficit to 10 percent of the gross domestic product

    B (p. 660)

38. The power to raise or lower the tax rate is part of
    A. fiscal policy.
    B. monetary policy.
    C. the contracting power.
    D. discretionary spending policy.

    A (p. 659)

39. A tax on imported goods is called a
    A. regressive tax.
    B. public good.
    C. tariff.
    D. monopoly tax.

    C (p. 661)

40. Before World War II, what was the federal government's most important source of revenue?
    A. personal income taxes
    B. corporate taxes
    C. excise taxes
    D. user fees

    C (p. 662)

41. When people in the lower income brackets pay a larger percentage of their income toward a tax, it is called _____ taxation.
    A. progressive
    B. regressive
    C. inflationary
    D. redistributive

    B (p. 662)

42. Sales taxes are _____, and most income taxes are _____.
    A. regressive, regressive
    B. progressive, progressive
    C. progressive, regressive
    D. regressive, progressive

    D (p. 662)

43. A(n) _____ is an incentive in the tax code to individuals and corporations to invest their money in ways the government desires, in exchange for a reduction in tax liabilities.
    A. categorical grant
    B. loophole
    C. federal fund rate
    D. open market operation

    B (p. 663)

44. The _____ is determined by the amount government spending exceeds government revenue in a fiscal year.
    A. budget deficit
    B. inflation rate
    C. gross domestic product
    D. reserve requirement

    A (p. 665)

45. Which of the following is NOT an example of mandatory spending?
    A. farm price supports
    B. Social Security payments
    C. defense spending
    D. Medicare

    C (p. 665)

46. Approximately what percentage of the federal budget is made up of uncontrollables?
    A. 25 percent
    B. 35 percent
    C. 65 percent
    D. 90 percent

    C (p. 665)

47. _____ policies are designed to eliminate the abuses of powerful _____.
    A. Redistributive, tariffs
    B. Fiscal, loopholes
    C. Antitrust, monopolies
    D. Taxation, gross domestic product indexes.

    C (p. 667)

48. The most consistently powerful nongovernment actors in determining economic policy are
    A. labor unions.
    B. environmental groups.
    C. business organizations.
    D. foreign nations.

    C (p. 674)

TRUE OR FALSE

1. The theory of laissez-faire argues that economic growth increases when government leaves the marketplace alone.

    T (p. 645)

2. Keynesian economics argues that government involvement in economic regulation is an unwarranted restriction on individual liberty.

    F (p. 646)

3. Inflation in the United States has maintained a steady rate of 11 percent for the past two decades.

    F (p. 651)

4. All tariffs in the United States have been eliminated since the Great Depression.

    F (p. 654)

5. The Federal Reserve Board is the chief institution for the establishment of monetary policy.

    T (p. 660)

6. A tax on a pack of cigarettes is a regressive tax.

    T (p. 662)

7. Less than one-quarter of the federal budget consists of mandatory spending priorities.

    F (p. 665)

8. Economic subsidies were first introduced in the United States during the 1930s.

    F (p. 672)

9. Historically, Americans have been more concerned with economic liberty than economic equality.

T (p. 675)

CHAPTER 17 | Social Policy

MULTIPLE CHOICE

1. Which of the following is not a goal of American social policy?
   A. the alleviation of poverty
   B. the promotion of equality of opportunity
   C. closing the gap between rich and poor
   D. protecting people against risks such as disability, illness, and unemployment

   C (p. 685)

2. The goals of American social policy are
   A. popular and receive wide support.
   B. often controversial.
   C. determined not by popular opinion but by the Constitution.
   D. often changed drastically from administration to administration.

   B (p. 686)

3. The goals of social policy
   A. are often reactions to social and economic events in the United States.
   B. have been consistent since the early twentieth century.
   C. are determined by the political party that controls the White House.
   D. All of the above.

   A (pp. 685–86)

209

4. Who was in charge of caring for the poor during the nineteenth century?
   A. local government
   B. the federal government
   C. private charities
   D. A and C

   D (p. 687)

5. When was the beginning of the American welfare state?
   A. 1890s
   B. 1930s
   C. 1960s
   D. 1980s

   B (p. 687)

6. What was the primary problem with private charities before the development of the welfare state?
   A. They would make subjective decisions on who was deserving or undeserving of aid.
   B. They were unable to get the necessary government licenses to operate legally.
   C. They disrupted the constitutional separation of church and state.
   D. All of the above.

   A (p. 687)

7. What was outdoor relief distributed by private charities?
   A. a place to sleep at night
   B. a temporary job
   C. money
   D. a ticket out of town

   C (p. 687)

8. What was the main fear concerning the consequences of outdoor relief?
   A. It perpetuated poverty.
   B. It was not cost effective.
   C. It involved the state too much.
   D. It was unconstitutional.

   A (p. 687)

9. Which group was the first to receive government assistance throughout the United States?
   A. African Americans, after the Civil War
   B. mothers with dependent children

C. the unemployed
D. newly arriving immigrants

B (p. 688)

10. How did the Great Depression change American attitudes about welfare?
    A. It showed that the government could efficiently distribute public assistance.
    B. It demonstrated that the government could choose between the deserving and undeserving poor in a more objective manner than private charities.
    C. It revealed that poverty could be caused by a flawed economic system, not just by personal irresponsibility.
    D. It revealed that local governments were too corrupt to be trusted with welfare policies.

    C (p. 688)

11. When was Social Security established?
    A. 1897
    B. 1929
    C. 1935
    D. 1965

    C (p. 689)

12. Social Security is a good example of
    A. outdoor relief.
    B. indoor relief.
    C. a contributory program.
    D. a noncontributory program.

    C (p. 690)

13. Which of the following is NOT a program of forced savings?
    A. Social Security
    B. Medicare
    C. Temporary Assistance to Needy Families
    D. All of the above are forms of forced savings.

    C (p. 690)

14. The periodic adjustment of benefits or wages that takes into account the increased cost of living is called
    A. means testing.
    B. indexing.
    C. graphing.
    D. economic tabulating.

    B (p. 691)

15. A cost of living adjustment is based on what?
    A. the financing approved by Congress during each session
    B. the rate of inflation
    C. the relationship between the level of the federal deficit compared to the nation's gross national product
    D. the changing need of each recipient

    B (p. 691)

16. Which of the following statements about noncontributory programs is FALSE?
    A. Eligibility for these programs is determined through means testing.
    B. These programs may provide public housing, food stamps, and school lunches.
    C. The existence of these programs dates from the Civil War.
    D. These programs underwent drastic reform in the 1990s.

    C (p. 692)

17. Medicare is a _____ program; Medicaid is a _____ program.
    A. noncontributory, contributory
    B. contributory, noncontributory
    C. contributory, contributory
    D. noncontributory, noncontributory

    B (pp. 690, 692)

18. When potential recipients of a benefit must establish their genuine need, the government program is called
    A. indexed.
    B. contributory
    C. means tested.
    D. in kind.

    C (p. 692)

19. Which of the following programs provides an in-kind benefit?
    A. Supplemental Security Income (SSI)
    B. food stamps
    C. Medicare
    D. Temporary Assistance to Needy Families

    B (p. 692)

20. The Temporary Assistance to Needy Families program is administered
    A. by the federal government.
    B. by the states, with uniform benefit levels set by the federal government.
    C. by the states, with benefit levels varying between states.
    D. through private agencies, with governmental contracts.

    C (p. 692)

21. How is an entitlement different from a right?
    A. Unlike an entitlement, a right cannot be taken away by an act of Congress.
    B. Unlike a right, an entitlement can be revoked without the due process of law.
    C. Unlike an entitlement, only citizens have rights.
    D. All of the above.

    A (p. 693)

22. What was the significance of the Supreme Court case *Goldberg v. Kelly*?
    A. It established the right of noncitizens to public assistance.
    B. It held that public assistance benefits could not be revoked without due process of law.
    C. It held that the unequal welfare benefits were a violation of the equal protection clause.
    D. It allowed the executive branch, rather than Congress, to set public assistance rates.

    B (p. 693)

23. What do public opinion polls reveal about welfare policies?
    A. They receive widespread support, as long as they are means tested.
    B. They are among the most-disliked government programs.
    C. Their popularity is low but has been steadily climbing since the 1970s.
    D. The public support for welfare goes up when they are administered by the states.

    B (p. 694)

24. The welfare reforms of 1996 did all of the following EXCEPT
    A. place time limitations on how long a recipient could receive benefits.
    B. grant block grants to the states to fund the programs.
    C. restrict most legal immigrants from receiving benefits.
    D. take the federal government out of welfare policy, granting all authority to the states.

    D (p. 695)

25. Which of the following can be concluded from the results of the 1996 welfare reform?
    A. The reforms have done little to get people off of welfare dependency.
    B. The reforms have reduced the number of people on welfare but have done little to reduce poverty.
    C. The reforms have led to a reduction in overall poverty.
    D. The reforms have led to an increase in the number of welfare recipients.

    B (p. 696)

214 | Chapter 17

26. Approximately what percentage of the current federal budget is spent on uncontrollables, such as Social Security and Medicare?
    A. 20 percent
    B. 35 percent
    C. 65 percent
    D. 75 percent

    C (p. 696)

27. Over the past three decades, the level of federal payroll tax has _____, and the level of federal corporate taxes has _____.
    A. risen, risen
    B. fallen, fallen
    C. risen, fallen
    D. fallen, risen

    C (p. 696)

28. Which of the following social policies is the most costly to the government?
    A. Social Security
    B. food stamps
    C. public housing assistance
    D. Temporary Assistance to Needy Families

    A (p. 696)

29. Which of the following is NOT an identifiable problem with Social Security?
    A. As the work force gets older, the government will be forced to spend more on Social Security entitlements.
    B. The investment made in Social Security will soon fall below the interest available in an insured bank account.
    C. The political consensus supporting a federal retirement program is crumbling.
    D. The government is projected to experience shortfalls in the Social Security Trust Fund within a generation.

    C (p. 696)

30. Which of the following groups receives the most benefits from government's social policies?
    A. the middle class
    B. the working poor
    C. children
    D. racial and ethnic minorities

    A (p. 709)

Social Policy | 215

31. Which of the following groups receive the least benefits from government's social policies?
    A. the middle class
    B. children
    C. the elderly
    D. the wealthy

    B (p. 710)

32. Which of the following LEAST explains why the elderly receive a large share of social benefits?
    A. The elderly make up a large population.
    B. The elderly are perceived as deserving benefits.
    C. The elderly have developed strong interest groups and lobbying techniques.
    D. Most members of Congress are themselves elderly or soon will be.

    D (p. 710)

33. What is the shadow welfare state?
    A. the welfare that is distributed by local governments and special districts
    B. social benefits that are distributed by private employers who are being subsidized by the government
    C. the welfare payments that the government is committed to paying in the future
    D. private charities that have filled the gap left by reductions in government spending

    B (p. 711)

34. Which of the following is the best example of the shadow welfare state?
    A. soup kitchens supported by local churches
    B. food stamps
    C. workplace medical insurance
    D. cost of living adjustments

    C (p. 711)

35. _____ are programs where the government provides a tax deduction for spending on health insurance and other benefits by both employers and employees.
    A. Noncompulsory benefits
    B. Tax expenditures
    C. Direct services
    D. Earned income tax credits

    B (p. 711)

36. Which of the following is NOT a reason why the working poor receive such a small amount of social policy benefits?
    A. They are often too poor to enjoy the subsidies of the shadow welfare state.
    B. Because they are employed, they cannot receive assistance through Temporary Assistance for Needy Families.
    C. The working poor are not a well-organized political force.
    D. The working poor are often seen as undeserving by public opinion.

    D (p. 713)

37. Which of the following programs most benefits the working poor?
    A. earned income tax credits
    B. Medicaid
    C. Temporary Assistance for Needy Families
    D. subsidized student loans

    A (p. 712)

38. Since the welfare reforms of 1996, what is the primary reason for receiving federal cash assistance if one is nonworking and able bodied?
    A. The recipient is caring for children.
    B. The recipient is going to school or in a job-training program.
    C. The recipient has been means tested.
    D. The recipient has been considered deserving.

    A (p. 713)

39. Since the mid-1990s, by what percentage range have the number of welfare recipients declined in the United States?
    A. between 5 and 10 percent
    B. between 20 and 30 percent
    C. between 50 and 60 percent
    D. between 80 and 90 percent

    C (p. 714)

40. Which of the following statements is INCORRECT?
    A. Women are more likely to be poor than men.
    B. African Americans have experienced twice as much unemployment as other Americans.
    C. The poverty rates for African Americans and Hispanic Americans are triple that of non-Hispanic white Americans.
    D. All of the above are correct.

    D (pp. 714–15)

41. Which of the following is NOT a reason why single mothers are more than twice as likely as other Americans to be below the poverty line?
    A. Child care adds a costly expense to the family budget.

B. Women make on average less than men.
   C. Many women in low-wage jobs do not have health insurance benefits.
   D. There have never been lobbying groups for single mothers.

   D (p. 714)

42. What is the most significant force determining the distribution of opportunities in the United States?
    A. education
    B. level of wealth
    C. race
    D. physical beauty

    A (p. 699)

43. What was the most significant educational policy developed by the federal government in the nineteenth century?
    A. the creation of compulsory public education
    B. the establishment of land grant colleges
    C. the creation of the G.I. Bill
    D. the development of a standard national elementary school curriculum

    B (p. 699)

44. What event brought federal attention to elementary school education?
    A. the fear that the Soviets were winning the cold war through better technology
    B. the low levels of literacy in America's inner cities
    C. the return of veterans at the end of World War II
    D. the Great Depression

    A (p. 699)

45. Which president styled himself as the education president?
    A. Lyndon B. Johnson
    B. Ronald Reagan
    C. Bill Clinton
    D. George H. W. Bush

    D (p. 702)

46. Since the 1930s American employment and training programs have
    A. been highly successful.
    B. fared poorly in terms of both expense and results.
    C. been more successful than similar attempts in Europe.
    D. varied in success depending on which state administered them.

    B (p. 706)

47. What was the result of the efforts to reform health care in the United States in 1994?
    A. A law was passed granting almost all Americans health care coverage.
    B. A law granting health care coverage to almost all Americans passed Congress but was vetoed by President Bill Clinton.
    C. A law increasing federal subsidies for health insurance to the working poor was passed and signed.
    D. Health care reform met resistance and no bill was voted on by Congress.

    D (p. 707)

48. _____ is the political philosophy that holds that government social programs are a potential threat to personal freedom.
    A. Liberalism
    B. Conservatism
    C. Libertarianism
    D. Socialism

    C (p. 716)

49. Who argues that most social problems are not the result of the economic system but rather a matter of individual responsibility?
    A. liberals
    B. conservatives
    C. socialists
    D. communists

    B (p. 717)

50. Where do most liberals see the source of most social problems?
    A. a lack of personal responsibility
    B. an unequally structured economy
    C. a large and irresponsible federal government
    D. state and local governments

    B (p. 717)

TRUE OR FALSE

1. The policy goal of alleviating poverty has been controversial in American society.

    T (p. 686)

2. The earliest form of public welfare in the United States was distributed by the individual states and paid for with property taxes.

    F (p. 687)

3. The Great Depression altered American attitudes about the causes and responsibility for poverty.

   T (p. 688)

4. Food stamps and Medicaid are both forms of contributory programs.

   F (p. 692)

5. The welfare reforms of 1996 gave much more administrative responsibility and authority to the states.

   T (p. 695)

6. Unlike a right, an entitlement can be taken away without due process of law.

   F (p. 693)

7. Spending on Social Security is difficult to control because benefits automatically go up along with the cost of living.

   T (p. 696)

8. The elderly and middle classes receive the largest share of benefits from social policies.

   T (p. 709)

9. American job training programs have had notable success.

   F (p. 706)

10. Libertarians argue that the United States has cut too many social policies over the past decade.

    F (p. 716)

CHAPTER 18 | Foreign Policy

MULTIPLE CHOICE

1. The primary task of the White House Office for Homeland Defense is to
   A. conduct the government's domestic war on terrorism.
   B. coordinate the intelligence activities and information among dozens of government agencies.
   C. coordinate the flow of intelligence between the United States and foreign nations.
   D. All of the above.

   B (pp. 725–26)

2. What is the main difference between a maker and a shaper of American foreign policy?
   A. Makers are those who have access to the president, as opposed to shapers.
   B. Shapers are those who draft the general goals of American policy, while makers are those specialists who concretely implement those goals.
   C. Makers are those within government, while shapers are influential groups outside of official government.
   D. Shapers are all domestic groups and institutions, while makers are foreign nations.

   C (p. 727)

3. Which of the following is the most important actor in the foreign policy establishment?
   A. Congress

B. the president
   C. Department of State
   D. Department of Defense

   B (p. 728)

4. Due to the rise of economic globalization, which office became increasing important in foreign policy during the 1990s under the leadership of Ron Brown?
   A. Secretary of Treasury
   B. Secretary of Commerce
   C. Joint Chiefs of Staffs
   D. National security adviser

   B (p. 728)

5. The most important task of the Senate in foreign policy is
   A. establishing embassies in foreign nations.
   B. ratifying the military budget.
   C. reviewing and approving treaties.
   D. declaring war.

   C (p. 729)

6. An agreement between the president and another country that has the force of a treaty but without congressional approval is called
   A. an executive memorandum.
   B. an executive agreement.
   C. an international protocol.
   D. an international accord.

   B (p. 730)

7. The North American Free Trade Agreement is
   A. a trade treaty between Mexico, Canada, and the United States designed to lower and eliminate tariffs.
   B. an executive agreement between the United States and the other nations of North and Central America, giving each other most favored nation trade status.
   C. a treaty between the United States, Canada, and Mexico, pledging a unified strategy regarding trade with Asia and Europe.
   D. an executive agreement reducing trade and immigration barriers throughout North America.

   A (p. 732)

8. How can Congress change or amend an executive agreement?
   A. Congress can do nothing to change or stop an executive agreement.
   B. Congress can veto an executive agreement.
   C. Congress can pass a joint resolution, revoking an executive agreement.
   D. The Senate has the power to approve or disapprove of all executive agreements.

   C (p. 731)

9. Which of the following American ethnic groups has the reputation for the greatest influence on American foreign policy?
   A. Chinese Americans
   B. Jewish Americans
   C. Italian Americans
   D. Mexican Americans

   B (p. 732)

10. What is the most difficult task for large foreign-policy-oriented interest groups?
    A. keeping members interested and active
    B. gaining access to the critical members of Congress and the White House
    C. maintaining enough control on its members to be capable of speaking with a unified voice
    D. avoiding the historical precedents against active lobbying on foreign policy subjects

    C (p. 732)

11. Which of the following does NOT represent an important interest reflected through the actions of foreign policy interest groups?
    A. ethnic solidarity
    B. promotion of economic interests
    C. human rights enforcement
    D. domestic representation of foreign governments

    D (p. 733)

12. Which of the following interest groups in the United States will more likely depend on demonstrations and other nontraditional strategies of influence?
    A. ethnic groups
    B. economic groups
    C. environmental groups
    D. human rights groups

    C (p. 733)

13. What is the most critical resource the media has to influence foreign policy?
    A. the ability to shape and direct public opinion in areas most Americans do not understand
    B. the speed and scale with which the media can spread political communication
    C. the ability to go to court to demand the release of information deemed classified
    D. the ability to set the agenda of foreign policy

    B (p. 733)

14. "Videomalaise" was a term coined to describe what phenomena?
    A. People no longer react with horror to violence, because they have seen it so often on television.
    B. People who rely on television as their main source of news tend to have negative attitudes toward government policies and officials.
    C. People tend to tune out of politics because they become saturated with news on the television.
    D. People spend so much time watching television they have no time left to keep up with the news.

    B (p. 733)

15. What eighteenth-century politician warned Americans against too much involvement with foreign nations?
    A. George Washington
    B. Thomas Jefferson
    C. John Adams
    D. Aaron Burr

    A (p. 735)

16. Nineteenth-century tariff policy is a good example of what enduring aspect of American foreign policy?
    A. the drive toward economic expansionism
    B. the desire for an isolationist position
    C. the intermingling of domestic and foreign policy
    D. the control of foreign policy by Wall Street

    C (p. 737)

17. The policy that seeks to avoid international alliances or commitments is called
    A. expansionism.
    B. Manifest Destiny.
    C. unilateralism.
    D. monetarism.

    C (p. 737)

18. What was the primary goal of American foreign policy in the nineteenth century?
    A. the competition for influence with European powers
    B. the creation of an overseas empire
    C. territorial expansion in North America
    D. the development of multilateralism with other nations in North and South America, to ward off European powers

    C (p. 737)

19. What was the most significant change in foreign affairs brought about by World War I?
    A. the destruction of the balance-of-power system between the major European powers
    B. the inheritance by the United States of a large overseas empire
    C. the rise of the United States as the only global superpower
    D. the active participation by the United States in the League of Nations

    A (p. 737)

20. When did the cold war begin?
    A. in the 1940s, soon after World War II
    B. in the early 1950s with the Korean War
    C. in the late 1950s, with American involvement in Vietnam
    D. in the early 1960s, with the Cuban Missile Crisis

    A (p. 737)

21. The North Atlantic Treaty Organization (NATO) is an example of
    A. mutually assured destruction.
    B. bilateralism.
    C. multilateralism.
    D. the domino theory.

    C (p. 737)

22. When was NATO formed?
    A. 1919
    B. 1941
    C. 1948
    D. 1956

    C (p. 737)

23. The policy to limit the expansion and influence of the Soviet Union was called
    A. isolationism.
    B. containment.

C. bilateralism.
D. the domino theory.

B (p. 737)

24. Which of the following was NOT a reflection of the American policy of containment?
    A. the Korean War
    B. the formation of NATO
    C. the formation of the United Nations
    D. the Vietnam War

    C (p. 737)

25. The most noteworthy example of the policy of deterrence was
    A. the Vietnam War.
    B. the Cuban Missile Crisis.
    C. the arms race.
    D. the Berlin blockade.

    C (p. 737)

26. The fall of the Soviet Union is best explained as
    A. the success of a policy of containment.
    B. the result of mutually assured destruction.
    C. the victory of capitalism over communism.
    D. the outmoded nature of federated empires.

    C (p. 737)

27. All of the following are elements of a nation-state EXCEPT
    A. its citizens must share a common political authority.
    B. its citizens must share a common cultural experience.
    C. it must be recognized by other sovereignties as a nation-state.
    D. it must be a member of the United Nations.

    D (p. 738)

28. The representation of a government to other foreign governments is called
    A. multilateralism.
    B. alliances.
    C. treaty.
    D. diplomacy.

    D (p. 739)

29. The traditional American distrust of diplomacy has resulted in which of the following situations?
   A. The budget and personnel at the State Department has been drastically cut since the end of the cold war.
   B. Presidents often use military or political leaders outside the State Department during a crisis.
   C. The United States has been closing down embassies in many nations since the mid-1990s.
   D. All of the above.

   B (p. 739)

30. The U.N. Security Council has _____ permanent members and _____ elected members.
   A. 5, 5
   B. 10, 10
   C. 5, 10
   D. 10, 25

   C (p. 742)

31. Which of the following nations does not have a permanent seat on the U.N. Security Council?
   A. United States
   B. Russia
   C. Germany
   D. United Kingdom

   C (p. 742)

32. Which of the following wars was conducted under the authority of the United Nations?
   A. World War II
   B. the Korean War
   C. the Vietnam War
   D. All of the above.

   B (p. 742)

33. Approximately what percentage of the United Nation's budget is paid for currently by the United States?
   A. 5 percent
   B. 10 percent
   C. 25 percent
   D. 50 percent

   C (p. 742)

34. In the immediate wake of 9/11, the U.N. Security Council unanimously passed a resolution
    A. supporting the United States's war on terrorism.
    B. requiring all nations to deny safe haven to terrorists or those who finance terrorism.
    C. authorizing the invasion of Afghanistan to remove the Taliban.
    D. offering a multimillion dollar reward for the capture of Osama bin Laden.

    B (p. 743)

35. Which of the following was the United Nations NOT involved in?
    A. World War II
    B. Persian Gulf War
    C. Bosnia
    D. weapons inspections in Iraq in 2002

    A (pp. 742–43)

36. What institution was established in 1944 to provide loans to needy member nations, to help overcome temporary trade deficits?
    A. the World Bank
    B. the Securities and Exchange Commission
    C. the International Monetary Fund
    D. the Department of Treasury

    C (p. 744)

37. The international institution designed in 1944 to help finance long-term capital investments is
    A. the World Bank.
    B. the Securities and Exchange Commission.
    C. the International Monetary Fund.
    D. the Department of Treasury.

    A (p. 744)

38. What critical international issue led U2 singer Bono and Secretary of Treasury Paul O'Neill to tour equatorial Africa in 2002?
    A. the need for debt relief in many third world nations
    B. the necessity of lower interest rates from the World Bank for the developing world
    C. the benefits of lower trade tariffs between the first and third worlds
    D. the importance of stamping out copyright piracy

    A (p. 745)

228 | Chapter 18

39. What was the Marshall Plan?
   A. the original blueprints for the United Nations
   B. the early attempt to establish a military alliance between North America and western Europe
   C. the economic recovery package of aid from the United States to western Europe after World War II
   D. the aid to rebuild the Japanese economy along capitalist lines after World War II

   C (p. 745)

40. Which of the following has NOT been a criticism of U.S. policy of distributing foreign aid?
   A. American aid largely goes to the political elite and not to the needy of the recipient nation.
   B. American aid programs have not been tied close enough to U.S. diplomacy.
   C. The United States gives a much larger percentage of its gross domestic product in foreign aid than European nations.
   D. All of the above are criticisms of U.S. foreign aid policy.

   C (pp. 745–46)

41. Of which of the following collective security organizations is the United States NOT a member?
   A. the Southeast Asia Treaty Organization
   B. the Warsaw Pact
   C. the Organization of American States
   D. A and C.

   B (pp. 746–47)

42. When Woodrow Wilson announced that "the world must be made safe for democracy," he was expressing the need for the United States to take on
   A. the Napoleonic role.
   B. the Holy Alliance role.
   C. the balance-of-power role.
   D. the economic expansionist role.

   A (p. 755)

43. The _____ role is pursued by nations attempting to preserve the social order against all revolutions and other major regime changes.
   A. Napoleonic
   B. Holy Alliance

C. balance-of-power
D. economic expansionist

B (p. 755)

44. U.S. policy in Central and Latin America can best be understood as a combination of which two roles?
    A. Napoleonic and Holy Alliance
    B. Napoleonic and economic expansionist
    C. Holy Alliance and economic expansionist
    D. Holy Alliance and balance-of-power

    C (p. 756)

45. What event most dramatically altered America's cold war bipolar view of world power?
    A. the Cuban Missile Crisis
    B. the Vietnam War
    C. the American recognition of communist China
    D. the Iranian revolution

    C (p. 757)

46. When many different ethnic nationalities demand self-determination and sovereignty, this process is known as
    A. multilateralism.
    B. the New World Order.
    C. Balkanization.
    D. revolutionary insurrection.

    C (p. 757)

47. Protests against the World Trade Organization (WTO) in recent years are best understood as a reaction against
    A. debt relief for third world nations.
    B. the local effects of economic globalization.
    C. American military and economic hegemony.
    D. opening trade relations with China.

    B (p. 759)

48. The phenomenon of _____ refers to conflicts within a nation-state between those benefiting from and those hurt by globalization.
    A. internal bipolarity
    B. external unilateralism
    C. balance of power
    D. internal deterrence

    A (p. 759)

49. Which of the following is NOT an example of the United States playing a Holy Alliance role?
    A. the Gulf War of 1991
    B. helping to oust the Haitian military dictators in 1994
    C. the Bosnia peace-keeping mission beginning in 1995
    D. All of the above are examples of the Holy Alliance role.

    B (pp. 760–62)

50. Which of the following places has the United States NOT militarily intervened in during the 1990s?
    A. Haiti
    B. Kosovo
    C. Iraq
    D. Uruguay

    D (pp. 760–64)

TRUE OR FALSE

1. Congress is the most important maker of American foreign policy.

   F (p. 727)

2. Domestic ethnic interest groups have exerted a powerful influence on American foreign policy toward the country of their national origin.

   T (p. 732)

3. Historically, Americans have made a sharp distinction between foreign and domestic policy.

   F (pp. 736–37)

4. NATO and the United Nations have been important instruments of American unilateralism.

   F (p. 737)

5. The United States has had a distrust of traditional methods of diplomacy in foreign relations.

   T (p. 739)

6. Throughout its history, the United Nations has always been a critical check on American foreign policy goals.

   F (p. 742)

7. Until after World War II, American policy was to demobilize the military during times of peace.

    T (p. 751)

8. Attempts by the United States to overthrow unfriendly regimes demonstrate a recent commitment to the balance-of-power role.

    F (p. 755)

9. The policy of containment shows the United States in a Holy Alliance role.

    T (p. 756)

10. The active use of the Holy Alliance role has made diplomacy no longer necessary for achieving American foreign policy goals.

    F (p. 764)

CHAPTER 19 | The Political Culture, People, and Economy of Texas

MULTIPLE CHOICE

1. Traditionalistic political cultures, according to Daniel Elazar, are typically found in
   A. the Northeast.
   B. the West.
   C. the South.
   D. the Midwest.

   C (p. 775)

2. A belief that government is designed to promote the public good describes the _____ political culture.
   A. traditionalistic
   B. moralistic
   C. individualistic
   D. All of the above.

   B (p. 775)

3. Which of the following would best characterize a traditionalistic individualistic political culture?
   A. low taxes and deference to business leaders
   B. government policies that promote traditional social morals
   C. government policies designed to benefit the political elite
   D. encouragement of active participation in government

   A (p. 775)

4. Which of the following is the best description of Texan political culture?
   A. Texas currently resembles the U.S. West more than the South in terms of its political culture.

B. Texans have a moralistic political culture.
C. The political culture of Texas has been dominated by Hispanic immigration.
D. Texas has multiple political cultures within its borders.

D (p. 776)

5. Which of the following does NOT reflect one of the historic characteristics that make up Texan political culture?
   A. provincialism
   B. the dominance of business interests
   C. the strong role of labor unions
   D. the dominance of the Democratic Party

   C (pp. 776–78)

6. Provincialism is best defined as
   A. the belief that God will lead.
   B. a narrow view of the world.
   C. the belief in limited government.
   D. the belief in the free market.

   B (p. 777)

7. Which of the following has traditionally dominated the political culture of Texas?
   A. labor unions
   B. business interests
   C. environmentalist groups
   D. the Catholic Church

   B (p. 777)

8. Which of the following political groups have traditionally had the least influence on Texas politics?
   A. labor unions
   B. business groups
   C. trial lawyers
   D. Mexican-American interest groups

   A (p. 777)

9. Houston is to be found in the Texas
   A. interior lowlands.
   B. Great Plains.
   C. Basin and Range Province.
   D. Gulf coastal plains.

   D (p. 779)

10. Which city is located in the Great Plains region of Texas?
    A. Lubbock
    B. Fort Worth
    C. El Paso
    D. San Antonio

    A (p. 780)

11. Creative destruction in Texas is best evidenced by
    A. the Civil War's positive effect on the Texas economy.
    B. the boom and bust cycle of the oil industry.
    C. the development of a high-tech industry after a slump in oil prices.
    D. the continued reliance on ranching.

    C (p. 782)

12. By 1998, approximately what percentage of Texans lived on farms or ranches?
    A. 2 percent
    B. 10 percent
    C. 18 percent
    D. 25 percent

    A (p. 784)

13. Which of the following did NOT contribute to the spread of cattle ranching in the nineteenth century?
    A. the invention of barbed wire
    B. the rationalization of cattle raising techniques
    C. the antigrazing position of farm unions
    D. the development of large and economically diverse ranches

    C (p. 783)

14. When in Texas history did cattle become big business?
    A. during the period of Mexican rule
    B. during the Republic
    C. after the Civil War
    D. from the 1930s to the 1950s

    C (p. 783)

15. Currently, how much of domestically produced cotton comes from Texas?
    A. 1/10
    B. 1/4
    C. 1/2
    D. 3/5

    B (p. 784)

16. _____ was the chief economic product of Texas during the early twentieth century.
    A. cattle
    B. cotton
    C. oil
    D. manufacturing

    C (p. 784)

17. What event occurred at Spindletop, Texas?
    A. Oil was discovered.
    B. The first free-range ranch in Texas was established.
    C. The last battle for Texan independence was fought.
    D. The state's worst race riots occurred.

    A (p. 784)

18. NAFTA established
    A. free trade between North and Central America.
    B. free trade between Mexico, the United States, and Canada.
    C. free trade between Texas and Mexico.
    D. a more liberalized immigration policy.

    B (p. 791)

19. Approximately what percentage of the population of Texas currently is Hispanic?
    A. 10 percent
    B. 30 percent
    C. 50 percent
    D. 65 percent

    B (p. 792)

20. In 1944, the Supreme Court case of *Smith v. Allwright* ended
    A. school segregation.
    B. poll taxes.
    C. white primaries.
    D. black codes.

    C (p. 797)

21. Which racial or ethnic group in Texas is concentrated in East Texas?
    A. Hispanics
    B. German Americans
    C. African Americans
    D. Asian Americans

    C (p. 797)

22. Which of the following statements regarding poverty is correct?
    A. Older populations tend to be poorer.
    B. Poverty grows at the same rate as urbanization.
    C. Texas has a low level of poverty compared with other states.
    D. The percentage of Texans living below the poverty line decreased only slightly in the 1990s.

    D (p. 799)

23. What was Stephen Austin's role in the development of Texas?
    A. He established the first free-range cattle ranch.
    B. He worked with the Spanish government to bring American settlers into Texas.
    C. He was an important early oil entrepreneur.
    D. He designed the city that bears his name.

    B (p. 800)

24. Which of the following statements regarding urbanization in Texas is incorrect?
    A. Texas has grown to be one of the most urbanized states in the Union.
    B. Historically, Texan urbanization depended on the spread of the railroad.
    C. The origins of cities in Texas are found in Native American civilizations.
    D. Urbanization has been less pronounced in West Texas than in the central and eastern regions of the state.

    C (pp. 800–801)

25. Which city in Texas currently has the largest population?
    A. San Antonio
    B. Dallas
    C. Houston
    D. El Paso

    C (p. 801)

TRUE OR FALSE

1. Texas political culture is best described as moralistic political.

   F (p. 776)

2. Throughout its history, business interests have dominated Texas's political culture.

   T (p. 777)

3. Houston is located in the Gulf coastal plains region.

   T (p. 779)

4. Agriculture accounts for 35 percent of the contemporary Texan workforce.

   F (p. 784)

5. Oil was the primary industry in Texas during the nineteenth century.

   F (p. 784)

6. Oil was first discovered in West Texas in 1842.

   F (p. 784)

7. In Texas today, the high-tech industry accounts for the greatest percentage of the state's exports.

   T (p. 790)

8. NAFTA has created a free trade market throughout North and Central America.

   F (p. 791)

9. People of Hispanic origin make up over 30 percent of Texas's population today.

   T (p. 792)

10. The largest city in Texas is San Antonio.

    F (p. 801)

CHAPTER 20 | The Texas Constitution

MULTIPLE CHOICE

1. Which of the following is NOT a function of state constitutions?
   A. to create political institutions and explain what their powers are
   B. to prevent concentrations of too much power in one office, through a series of checks and balances
   C. to set the proper tax rates for state and county authorities
   D. to forbid certain government actions, by establishing civil liberties

   C (p. 812)

2. The supremacy clause of the U.S. Constitution states that
   A. the constitution of Texas is the supreme law in Texas.
   B. laws passed by the national government are supreme over all state laws.
   C. the president is the supreme government authority throughout the United States.
   D. all laws passed by the Texas legislature are supreme, even if they conflict with federal laws.

   B (p. 812)

3. The system of distributing powers between states and a central government is called
   A. federalism.
   B. separation of powers.
   C. constitutionalism.
   D. filtration.

   A (p. 812)

4. Which of the following is the best definition of a confederation?
   A. a system of government where states maintain their sovereignty, except in those powers they have expressly delegated to the national government
   B. a system of government where all political power granted by the people is clearly expressed in a constitution, making a written bill of rights unnecessary
   C. a system of government in which the national government has extensive powers over the states
   D. a system of government that permits slavery

   A (p. 813)

5. What is the most important difference between the Constitution of the United States and state constitutions?
   A. Most state constitutions create confederated forms of government.
   B. Civil rights are not to be found in state constitutions.
   C. The U.S. Constitution contains no checks and balances.
   D. States are subordinate to the federal government.

   D (pp. 812–13)

6. Which of the following describes an important part of the 1827 constitution of *Coahuila y Tejas,* established when Texas was part of Mexico?
   A. The constitution of *Coahuila y Tejas* established Catholicism as an official religion.
   B. The constitution of *Coahuila y Tejas* established a unicameral legislature.
   C. The constitution of *Coahuila y Tejas* attempted to restrict the spread of slavery.
   D. All of the above.

   D (p. 814)

7. The main problem that stalled the admission of Texas into the United States was
   A. the lack of enough people in Texas.
   B. Texas's overly large debt, which would have to be assumed by the federal government.
   C. Texas would be a pro-slavery state.
   D. Mexico's refusal to concede to Texas's independence.

   C (p. 817)

8. The Texas constitutional convention of 1861 was dominated by
   A. lawyers and slaveholders.
   B. small farmers and ranchers.
   C. representatives of business and the railroads.
   D. supporters of Governor Sam Houston.

   A (p. 820)

9. The Texas constitution of 1869 was created
   A. because Texas needed a new constitution when it joined the Confederacy.
   B. by members of the Texas Republican Party.
   C. in order to limit the power of state government.
   D. as a reaction against Reconstruction.

   B (p. 821)

10. Who were the Radical Republicans?
    A. those Republicans who proposed to write a new U.S. constitution in the late 1990s
    B. Republicans after the Civil War who controlled Reconstruction policy in the former Confederate states
    C. those first Republicans since Reconstruction in Texas, during the 1960s, to win elected office
    D. followers of the pro-Union governor Sam Houston

    B (p. 821)

11. Which of the following was NOT part of E. J. Davis's post–Civil War governorship?
    A. the political domination of the Republicans
    B. the centralization of executive power in the governor's office
    C. the support of ex-Confederate soldiers
    D. the intimidation of political opponents

    C (pp. 821–23)

12. In what year was Texas's current constitution ratified?
    A. 1828
    B. 1845
    C. 1876
    D. 1999

    C (p. 823)

13. Who made up the Grange, and what effect did they have on the writing of the Texas constitution?
    A. They were a consortium of railroad entrepreneurs who wanted a constitution that would aid business interests.

B. They were a group of pro-Union Republicans who controlled the state after the Civil War.
C. They were an agricultural group who wanted a government that would improve the plight of farmers.
D. They were early wildcatters who wanted land grants from the state so they could explore for oil.

C (p. 823)

14. What principle of government is the key to understanding the drafting of the Texas constitution of 1876?
    A. the need for governmental subsidy and regulation of economic growth
    B. the importance of civil right protections for African Americans and Latinos
    C. the necessity of strong limitations on the authority of state officials
    D. the value of states' rights

    C (p. 823)

15. Which of the following was NOT a goal for those writing the Texas constitution?
    A. restrictions on the power of the government to get into debt
    B. limits on the ability of the government to tax
    C. checking the powers of the governor
    D. giving independence to the judiciary by making all judges appointed, instead of elected

    D (pp. 823–25)

16. What is the major difference between the Bill of Rights in the Texas constitution and the U.S. Bill of Rights?
    A. There is no Bill of Rights in the Texas constitution.
    B. The Texas constitution grants to Texans rights that are not found in the U.S. Constitution.
    C. The Texas Bill of Rights is far less detailed than the federal Bill of Rights.
    D. The Texas constitution has no specific rights for those accused of a crime.

    B (p. 826)

17. The separation of government into three branches—legislative, executive, and judicial—is called
    A. division of labor.
    B. checks and balances.
    C. separation of power.
    D. federalism.

    C (p. 827)

18. Which of the following statements best describes the structure of the Texas legislature?
    A. Ever since independence from Mexico, Texas has had a bicameral legislature.
    B. Texas's first unicameral legislature was established while the state was a member of the Confederacy.
    C. Texas has always had a unicameral legislature.
    D. One of the complaints against the Reconstruction constitution was that it created a unicameral legislature.

    A (p. 827)

19. Which of the following describes a significant difference between the structure of the Texas executive and the structure of the U.S. executive?
    A. In Texas, the executive is made up of several elected offices, instead of just one.
    B. The chief executive in Texas does not have the power to check the legislature with a veto, as the U.S. president can.
    C. The governor has term limits, while the U.S. president does not.
    D. The governor of Texas is paid more than the U.S. president.

    A (p. 828)

20. Under the Texas constitution, who has the power of impeachment?
    A. The House of Representatives has the power to impeach, while the Senate has the power to try and convict.
    B. The Senate has the power to both impeach and convict.
    C. The House of Representatives has the power to impeach, while the state Supreme Court has the power to try and convict.
    D. Texas has no constitutional provisions for impeachment.

    A (p. 830)

21. The Texas constitution requires which of the following for amendment?
    A. a two-thirds vote in both houses of the state legislature
    B. a majority vote from the voters of Texas
    C. the governor's signature
    D. A and B

    D (p. 831)

22. Approximately how often has the Texas constitution been amended?
    A. fewer than 30 times
    B. between 50 and 75
    C. between 400 and 425 times
    D. over 750 times

    C (p. 832)

23. What was the main criticism of the current Texas constitution behind the Ratliff-Junell proposal for a new constitution?
    A. The constitution gave the executive branch too much power over the legislative process.
    B. The constitution allowed for too many corrupt interest groups to control Texas politics.
    C. A new constitution should be drafted at least every century in order for it to be representative of the people.
    D. The constitution is too restrictive and cumbersome for contemporary government.

    D (p. 833)

24. Which of the following was NOT part of the Ratliff-Junell proposal for Texas constitutional change?
    A. The judiciary should be appointed by the governor, with confirmation by the Senate.
    B. The executive branch should be reorganized to look more like the U.S. presidency.
    C. The salaries of politicians should be increased.
    D. The length of terms of office would grow, but there would also be term limits.

    A (p. 833)

25. The Texas constitution is
    A. a tightly argued, brief document of general principles.
    B. a long, complex, and often overly detailed document.
    C. difficult to amend, compared to the federal constitution.
    D. an economic treatise disguised as a blueprint for government.

    B (p. 834)

TRUE OR FALSE

1. The current Texas constitution has been amended over 400 times.

   T (p. 825)

2. The state of Texas has had three constitutions in the course of its history.

   F (p. 812)

3. Controversy about admitting a new slave state held up the annexation of Texas into the United States for nine years.

   T (p. 817)

4. The Texas constitution of 1869 was written by members of the Republican Party, including ten African Americans.

   T (p. 821)

5. Urban business interests had the greatest role in writing the Texas constitution of 1876.

   F (p. 823)

6. The Texas constitution of 1876 was designed to limit the power of government, especially of the governor's office.

   T (p. 823)

7. Texas has a Bill of Rights containing more liberties than those found in the U.S. Bill of Rights.

   T (p. 826)

8. The Texas constitution created a unicameral legislature.

   F (p. 827)

9. The Texas constitution created a plural executive, consisting of multiple elected officers.

   T (p. 828)

10. There has been little serious attempt in recent years to change the Texas constitution.

    F (p. 831)

CHAPTER 21 | Parties and Elections in Texas

MULTIPLE CHOICE

1. The most important role for political parties in elections is to
   A. fund the candidates' campaigns.
   B. offer the candidates a label by which they can identify with the voters.
   C. lead get-out-the-vote drives.
   D. create political action committees.

   B (p. 844)

2. The most local voting district is called the
   A. precinct.
   B. county.
   C. district.
   D. caucus.

   A (p. 844)

3. Which party dominated Texas politics throughout most of the twentieth century?
   A. Democrats
   B. Republicans
   C. Populists
   D. Texas politics was nonpartisan for most of the twentieth century.

   A (p. 846)

4. In the 1950s, who were known as the Shivercrats?
   A. supporters of Governor Alan Shivers's bid for the White House in 1952 and 1956
   B. conservative Democrats who voted for Republican presidential candidates
   C. liberal Republicans who supported Democrat Alan Shivers's governorship
   D. poor rural Democrats who could not afford to buy heating oil because of soaring energy costs

   D (p. 846)

5. In Texas, why were primary elections more important than general elections during most of the twentieth century?
   A. The general election was often fixed.
   B. The primary election was the only election held in many Texas counties.
   C. The primary election was open to more voters than the general election.
   D. In a one-party state, the winner of the primary will most likely win the general election.

   D (p. 847)

6. The pattern, beginning in the 1950s, of Texans voting for a Republican president but sticking with conservative Democrats for state offices is called
   A. yellow dog democracy.
   B. presidential Republicanism.
   C. the white primary.
   D. the Eisenhower syndrome.

   B (p. 847)

7. Today, approximately, what is the level of party identity in Texas?
   A. The electorate is almost evenly divided between Republicans, Democrats, and independents.
   B. Texas continues to have significantly more self-identified Democrats than Republicans.
   C. Over 10 percent more Texan voters identify with the Republican Party than with the Democratic Party.
   D. Under a quarter of the voters are willing to identify with any party.

   A (p. 849)

8. Which of the following is NOT currently a common constituency group of the Democratic Party of Texas?
   A. African Americans
   B. the elderly

C. those new to Texas
  D. Hispanic Americans

  C (p. 851)

9. Suburban counties in Texas are more likely to have
   A. fewer registered voters than the Texas average.
   B. a Republican majority among voters
   C. suffered from a declining population.
   D. older, Democratic voters.

   B (p. 854)

10. The fastest growing demographic group in Texas is _____, who overwhelmingly vote for the _____ Party.
    A. Hispanics, Democratic
    B. whites, Democratic
    C. Hispanics, Republican
    D. African Americans, Republican

    A (p. 855)

11. When a voter must declare a party affiliation before the day of voting, this election is called
    A. an open primary.
    B. a closed primary.
    C. a special election.
    D. a convention.

    B (p. 857)

12. Which of the following is NOT a function of special elections?
    A. to choose which candidates will run in the general election
    B. to fill vacancies in elected offices
    C. to ratify amendments to the state constitution
    D. to give voter approval to borrow money

    A (p. 858)

13. John Nance Garner was
    A. a powerful lieutenant governor during the 1980s and 1990s.
    B. the first Republican senator from Texas since Reconstruction.
    C. a U.S. Speaker of the House from South Texas.
    D. a Texas governor during the 1910s who opposed women's suffrage.

    C (p. 859)

248 | Chapter 21

14. Which of the following was NOT regularly used in Texas as a method of disenfranchising many Texan minorities before the 1960s?
    A. the white primary
    B. early registration
    C. poll taxes
    D. All of the following were used in Texas.

    D (p. 859)

15. All of the following statements concerning white primaries are true EXCEPT
    A. they were designed to disenfranchise African Americans.
    B. the Democratic Party in Texas was established as a private, racially restricted club.
    C. the practice was declared illegal only with the Voting Rights Act of 1965.
    D. there were several Supreme Court cases regarding the white primary.

    C (pp. 859–60)

16. What is the significance of the Supreme Court case *Smith v. Allwright?*
    A. The Court declared the use of literacy tests a violation of the equal protection clause.
    B. The case compelled Texas to integrate Hispanic students into "whites only" public schools.
    C. It announced that, in primary elections, states could not restrict voters on account of race.
    D. It restricted the use of closed primaries.

    C (p. 860)

17. Which of the following is NOT a requirement to vote in Texas?
    A. U.S. citizenship
    B. must be at least eighteen years of age
    C. must be a resident of Texas for one year
    D. must be a resident of the county for thirty days

    C (p. 861)

18. The Motor Voter Act of 1993
    A. allows states to offer voters "drive-thru" voter booths.
    B. allows voters to register to vote while applying for a driver's license.
    C. restricts one's right to vote because of unpaid traffic tickets.
    D. was declared unconstitutional by the Supreme Court.

    B (p. 861)

19. The two most important factors that determine whether someone votes are
    A. age and income level.

B. income level and education.
   C. education and ethnicity.
   D. ethnicity and age.

   B (p. 863)

20. Early voting in Texas has been shown to produce
    A. a moderate increase in voter turnout.
    B. a significant increase in voter turnout.
    C. a moderate drop in voter turnout.
    D. a drastic drop in voter turnout.

    A (p. 864)

21. The elections of John Tower and Bill Clements demonstrate that
    A. ideological conflicts within the Democratic Party allowed the early Republican victories in statewide offices.
    B. in elections, money beats grassroots activism.
    C. the Republican Party had widespread support throughout the 1960s and 1970s.
    D. to succeed, Democrats need to win at least half of the Hispanic vote.

    A (p. 869)

22. What do data indicate about races for judicial offices throughout Texas?
    A. Television advertising makes little difference in the election.
    B. Television ads make a large impact in the election.
    C. Personal appearances, more than advertising, are the key to victory.
    D. Support by special interest groups, such as trial lawyers, is the key to electoral success.

    B (p. 868)

23. Who was the first Republican governor of Texas since Reconstruction?
    A. E. J. Davis
    B. William Clements
    C. Ann Richards
    D. George W. Bush

    B (p. 869)

24. Ann Richards
    A. became Texas's first female U.S. senator.
    B. was the last Democratic governor of Texas.
    C. is George W. Bush's secretary of transportation.
    D. was the powerful head of the state Republican Party during the 1990s.

    B (p. 876)

25. Which of the following is NOT a danger for the current Texas Republican Party?
    A. the rapid demographic growth of Hispanic Americans
    B. conflicts between religious conservatives and economic conservatives
    C. a decrease in the party's fund-raising
    D. the increasing number of Texan voters identifying as independent

    C (p. 878)

TRUE OR FALSE

1. The Republican Party has been the dominant force in Texas politics throughout most of the twentieth century.

    F (p. 846)

2. Beginning in the 1950s, Texan voters began to regularly split their ticket between Republicans and Democrats.

    T (p. 847)

3. Approximately 50 percent of Texan African Americans identify themselves as Republicans.

    F (p. 851)

4. Upper-income Texans are more likely to vote for the Democratic Party.

    F (p. 852)

5. Formally Texas has a closed primary, but in practice it is an open primary.

    T (p. 857)

6. Poll taxes, such as those used in Texas, disenfranchised poor voters.

    T (p. 859)

7. The Supreme Court declared the white primaries used in Texas were in violation of the U.S. Constitution.

    T (p. 860)

8. Texans tend to vote less than the national average.

    T (p. 861)

9. John Tower was the first Republican senator from Texas since the 1870s.

    T (p. 870)

10. Ann Richards lost her race for the governorship against Bill Clements in 1990.

    F (p. 875)

CHAPTER 22 | Interest Groups, Lobbying, and Lobbyists in Texas

MULTIPLE CHOICE

1. An interest group
   A. is designed to pursue a common goal.
   B. attempts to effect public policy.
   C. seeks to achieve its desired goals through political means.
   D. All of the above.

   D (p. 884)

2. The 8F Crowd was
   A. an influential cartel of political activists who wrote the Texas constitution of 1876.
   B. a loose but influential group of Texas businessmen.
   C. the first Latino civil rights organization in Texas.
   D. a group of corrupt politicians, during the early twentieth century, dependent on bribery.

   B (p. 884)

3. Which of the following is the farmers' interest group that influenced the writing of the Texas constitution of 1876?
   A. the Grange
   B. the 8F Group
   C. EMILY's List
   D. the Texas Natural Resource Council

   A (p. 884)

4. Interest groups are often powerful in states
   A. with a strong two-party rivalry.
   B. in states dominated by one party.
   C. in states that have a weak or nonexistent party system
   D. with powerful third parties.

   B (p. 884)

5. Which of the following is NOT a reason that interest groups are useful to politicians?
   A. Interest groups provide necessary information and expertise to politicians.
   B. Campaign funding often comes from interest groups.
   C. Interest groups provide politicians an agenda on which they may run for office.
   D. Interest groups can mobilize voters and mount publicity campaigns.

   C (p. 884)

6. The practice of combining several individual campaign contributions into one larger contribution from a group in order to increase the group's impact is known as
   A. bribery.
   B. PAC-ing.
   C. bundling.
   D. soft money.

   C (p. 885)

7. All of the following are benefits an interest group has over private citizens EXCEPT
   A. interest groups have staffs with greater expertise than one person can have.
   B. individuals often do not have the necessary time to lobby government.
   C. interest groups have greater legitimacy with politicians than citizens do.
   D. interest groups usually have access to more money and other material resources than individual citizens do.

   C (p. 885)

8. Corporate interest groups tend to use either _____ or _____ to represent their interests in Austin.
   A. government relations departments; law firms
   B. PACs; bundles
   C. the governor; members of the state legislature
   D. accountants; financial analysts

   A (p. 886)

9. The largest and most effective public employee interest group is the
   A. firefighters.
   B. police.
   C. teachers.
   D. justices of the peace.

   C (p. 886)

10. Which of the following is the best example of a public interest group?
    A. the Mexican American Legal Defense Fund
    B. the Texas Medical Association
    C. Common Cause
    D. Texans for Lawsuit Reform

    C (p. 886)

11. One important way for interest groups to gain access to those in Texas government is to employ _____ as lobbyists.
    A. retired sports stars
    B. political science majors
    C. Republican campaign consultants
    D. former legislators and government officials

    D (p. 888)

12. There are currently between _____ and _____ registered lobbyists in Texas.
    A. 500, 1,000
    B. 2,000, 2,500
    C. 5,000, 5,500
    D. 7,500, 8,000

    B (p. 888)

13. Bribery is
    A. a common problem with lobbyists.
    B. legal as long as the payoff is publicized.
    C. not a common problem in Texas today.
    D. most commonly offered in the form of steak dinners.

    C (p. 889)

14. Which interest is NOT represented in a list of the top interest groups in Texas?
    A. trial lawyers
    B. the environment
    C. the gas and oil industry
    D. public employees

    B (p. 890)

15. Texas has _____ laws dealing with lobbying by former government officials.
    A. no
    B. numerous
    C. weak
    D. strong

    C (p. 889)

16. The Texas Chemical Council PAC is known as
    A. CHEMPAC
    B. FREEPAC
    C. NOPAC
    D. TCCPAC

    B (p. 891)

17. _____ was the former Texas Speaker of the House who was indicted for taking an illegal gift from a law firm that specialized in collecting delinquent taxes for local governments.
    A. "Gib" Lewis
    B. "Pete" Laney
    C. Bill Ratliff
    D. Tom Craddick

    A (p. 889)

18. Most PAC spending in Texas represents
    A. business.
    B. labor.
    C. single-issue ideological organizations.
    D. consumers.

    A (p. 894)

19. Over 50 percent of all ideological PAC contributions in Texas come from _____
    A. school voucher advocates.
    B. the National Rifle Association.
    C. anti-abortion groups.
    D. the Democrats' and Republicans' PACs.

    D (p. 894)

20. Which of the following PACs spend the least amount of money in Texas elections?
    A. single-issue PACs
    B. labor unions

C. business groups
D. lawyers

B (p. 895)

21. As in the U.S. Congress, most campaign contributions in Texas go to _____
    A. incumbents.
    B. supporters of business interests.
    C. Republicans.
    D. political parties.

    A (p. 898)

22. What does it mean for an interest group to "get on the late train"?
    A. The group's lobbyists are unable to gain access to key politicians until after all opposing lobbyists have been heard.
    B. An interest group gives contributions after the election to a winning candidate the group had opposed.
    C. A PAC donates money for a candidate in the general election but not in the primaries.
    D. An interest group picks up on an issue only after public opinion polling shows a great deal of support.

    B (p. 898)

23. PACs representing trial lawyers most often contribute to
    A. pro-business politicians.
    B. Democrats.
    C. rural politicians.
    D. Republicans from suburban districts.

    B (p. 894)

24. Throughout the 1980s and 1990s, the success of trial lawyer groups has
    A. risen, along with the amount of campaign donations.
    B. declined, along with the amount of campaign donations.
    C. declined, despite a high level of campaign contributions.
    D. risen, despite a decrease in campaign spending.

    C (p. 906)

25. Which of the following statements concerning Texans for Lawsuit Reform (TLR) is incorrect?
    A. TLR represents the interests of trial lawyers' and plaintiffs' groups.
    B. TLR has succeeded in lobbying for limits on legal liability damages.
    C. TLR donates money largely to Republican candidates.
    D. All of the above are correct.

    A (p. 901)

TRUE OR FALSE

1. Gaining access to politicians through personal connections is a violation of Texas state laws.

   F (p. 885)

2. Interest groups are limited to lobbying the legislature; they cannot lobby executive agencies or the courts.

   F (p. 889)

3. Few large interest groups in Texas represent the environment.

   T (p. 890)

4. More money is spent in Texas by the communications industry than any other represented interest.

   F (p. 894)

5. Spending on issue advocacy ads by PACs need not be reported by a candidate.

   T (p. 893)

6. PACs help interest groups bundle campaign donations.

   T (p. 890)

7. Incumbents are most likely to receive large campaign contributions.

   T (p. 898)

8. Some interest groups, such as the Texas Chemical Council, hire over 200 lobbyists.

   T (p. 903)

9. Texans for Lawsuit Reform is a group successful at getting stronger consumer safety regulations.

   F (p. 901)

10. The Texas trial lawyers have had less success in their lobbying efforts over the past decade.

    T (p. 906)

CHAPTER 23 | The Texas Legislature

MULTIPLE CHOICE

1. In the Texas legislature, the House has _____ members and the Senate has _____ members.
   A. 435, 100
   B. 100, 25
   C. 150, 31
   D. 31, 150

   C (p. 912)

2. The requirements for holding office in the Texas legislature
   A. are minimal, in keeping with the idea that office holding should be open to most citizens.
   B. are stricter than those in the federal legislature, reflecting the belief that only the most qualified Texans deserve to serve.
   C. require one to be a citizen of Texas but not necessarily a citizen of the United States.
   D. are the same as in the U.S. Constitution.

   A (p. 913)

3. The typical Texas legislator is most likely to be
   A. a white woman with a professional degree.
   B. a white, affluent businessman.
   C. a working-class Hispanic woman.
   D. a middle-class African American lawyer.

   B (p. 913)

4. What is the yearly salary of a Texas representative?
   A. below $7,500
   B. between $10,000 and $25,000
   C. between $25,000 and $50,000
   D. above $50,000

   A (p. 914)

5. For how long does the Texas legislature meet?
   A. The legislature meets all year, with breaks for holidays and campaigning.
   B. The regular session is nine months, every year.
   C. The legislature meets for nine months, biennially.
   D. The regular legislative session lasts 140 days, every two years.

   D (p. 915)

6. The agenda for special sessions in the Texas legislature are set by
   A. the lieutenant governor and the Speaker of the House.
   B. the governor.
   C. the Texas Supreme Court.
   D. the chair of the joint committee on special sessions.

   B (p. 915)

7. What is the main difference between a bill and a resolution?
   A. A resolution is just another name for a bill.
   B. A resolution deals only with issues affecting local government, while a bill deals with all of the state.
   C. All bills require the signature of the governor, but no resolution does.
   D. Unlike a bill, a resolution, if passed, lacks the force of a public law.

   D (p. 916)

8. A bill in the Texas legislature that would allow a county to establish a new community college would be classified as a
   A. general bill.
   B. special bill.
   C. local bill.
   D. resolution.

   C (p. 916)

9. Constituency service provided by Texas representatives may include all of the following EXCEPT
   A. giving a speech to a local civic group.
   B. providing legal services in court.
   C. attempting to influence decisions of government agencies.
   D. writing a letter of recommendation for a constituent.

   B (p. 917)

10. Which of the following is NOT a nonlegislative power of the Texas legislature?
    A. the power of impeachment
    B. the power to investigate financial mismanagement in a state agency
    C. the power to formally count the election returns in the governor's race
    D. the power to overturn state Supreme Court decisions with a two-thirds majority

    D (p. 917)

11. In Texas, who can write a bill?
    A. only a member of the legislature
    B. the legislature or someone officially authorized by the legislature
    C. any government official
    D. anyone at all

    D (p. 918)

12. When, in 1957, Texas state senator Henry Gonzalez spoke for over twenty-two hours in opposition to a segregation bill, this was an example of
    A. a filibuster.
    B. standing committee work.
    C. cloture.
    D. floor action.

    A (p. 921)

13. As in the U.S. Congress, what is the purpose of a conference committee in the Texas legislature?
    A. It is a committee in which members of both houses meet informally with the governor's representatives to set the agenda for an upcoming session.
    B. It is a committee designed to make differing House and Senate versions of the same bill identical.
    C. It is the committee that establishes the rules for floor debate in the House.
    D. It is another name for a standing committee.

    B (p. 923)

14. When a committee chair "pigeonholes" a bill, what happens?
    A. The bill is set aside before it is ever discussed in committee.
    B. The bill is referred to a special session.
    C. The chair vetoes a bill after it has already received an affirmative committee vote.
    D. The chair refers a bill to only one subcommittee, rather than two or more.

    A (p. 921)

260 | Chapter 23

15. In Texas, why is a governor's postadjournment veto so powerful?
    A. It cannot be overturned by the legislature.
    B. It can be overturned only by a two-thirds majority of both houses.
    C. It allows the governor to veto parts of a bill but not all of it.
    D. It allows the governor to get maximum media coverage.

    A (p. 923)

16. When the governor strikes out specific spending provisions in large appropriations bills, this is called
    A. pigeonholing.
    B. the pocket veto.
    C. the line-item veto.
    D. the postadjournment veto.

    C (p. 923)

17. In Texas, which of the following determines what the legislature's agenda will be?
    A. the governor's priorities
    B. the stories and issues on which the media concentrates
    C. the influence of powerful lobbyists
    D. All of the above.

    D (pp. 924–27)

18. What is the most important check the governor has on the state legislature?
    A. the veto power
    B. the power to call special sessions
    C. the power to set the agenda for the legislative session
    D. the power to lobby members of the legislature

    A (p. 927)

19. Why is the comptroller of public accounts so important to the legislature?
    A. The comptroller is responsible for setting the salary and compensation packages for legislators.
    B. The comptroller informs the legislature how much money they have to spend on the budget.
    C. The comptroller investigates suspected illegal campaign contributions.
    D. Whoever is comptroller is also the Speaker of the House.

    B (p. 926)

20. Why isn't partisanship as important in the Texas legislature as it is in the U.S. Congress?
    A. Texas was essentially a single-party state until the 1980s.
    B. There is more ideological unity within Texas than throughout the United States.

C. The Texas legislature is more centralized than the U.S. Congress.
D. All of the above.

D (p. 929)

21. Which of the following is NEITHER a duty NOR a power of the lieutenant governor in Texas?
    A. the power to act as governor when the governor is away from the state
    B. the duty to preside over the Texas Senate
    C. the capacity to select the chairs of Texas Senate committees
    D. the ability to call the Texas Senate into special session

    D (pp. 928–29)

22. In the Texas House of Representatives, who has the power to allow members to speak in floor debates?
    A. the Speaker of the House
    B. the leader of the party to which the representative is a member
    C. the lieutenant governor
    D. House members do not need official permission to speak in floor debates.

    A (p. 930)

23. Legislative districts in the Texas House and Senate are
    A. based on proportional representation.
    B. single-member districts.
    C. multiple-member districts.
    D. redistricted every four years.

    B (p. 931)

24. Who has responsibility for redistricting the Texas delegation to the U.S. Congress?
    A. the Texas legislature
    B. the governor
    C. the governor, along with the Texas Senate
    D. the U.S. Congress

    A (p. 933)

25. What is the importance of the Supreme Court case *Reynolds v. Sims*?
    A. It declared the Voting Rights Act of 1965 constitutional.
    B. It declared poll taxes unconstitutional.
    C. It declared the constitutional principle of "one person, one vote."
    D. It declared that preclearance was an unconstitutional abridgement of state power.

    C (p. 932)

TRUE OR FALSE

1. The Texas legislature meets in regular session once every two years.

   T (p. 915)

2. The typical Texas legislator is a white, upper-class male Protestant.

   T (p. 913)

3. Special legislative sessions may last as long as it takes to complete the session's agenda.

   F (p. 915)

4. The House of Representatives is responsible for both impeaching government officials and holding the trial after impeachment.

   F (p. 917)

5. The governor's greatest legislative power is the appointment of the legislature's committee heads.

   F (p. 923)

6. The Texas constitution forbids the legislature to borrow money to conduct the daily operations of government.

   T (p. 926)

7. The lieutenant governor is also a member of the Texas House of Representatives.

   F (p. 928)

8. The Texas legislature has a lower level of partisanship than the U.S. Congress.

   T (p. 929)

9. Both the lieutenant governor and the Speaker of the House in Texas are elected in statewide elections.

   F (p. 928)

10. The secretary of state in Texas is responsible for redrawing legislative districts every ten years.

    F (p. 933)

CHAPTER 24 | The Texas Executive Branch

MULTIPLE CHOICE

1. The governor of Texas has
   A. strong formal powers granted by the Texas constitution.
   B. few formal powers, so the office is one of the weakest chief executives in the United States.
   C. the power to appoint all of the other officials in the executive branch.
   D. the power to appoint all state judges.

   B (p. 943)

2. In Texas, what is the primary effect of a plural executive?
   A. It dilutes the power of the governor and fragments the executive branch.
   B. It grants the governor additional powers, since it makes for a powerful executive branch.
   C. It makes the executive branch less accountable to the voters.
   D. It leads to excessive corruption within the executive branch.

   A (p. 943)

3. Why did the Texas constitution establish a plural executive?
   A. Texas was following the structure of the federal executive.
   B. There was suspicion of a strong chief executive after the Reconstruction governorship of E. J. Davis.
   C. The complications of running a state as large as Texas necessitate a plural executive.
   D. It was necessary in order for the executive branch to be as dominant as possible.

   B (p. 943)

4. How many women have been governor of Texas?
   A. none
   B. one
   C. two
   D. five

   C (p. 944)

5. In Texas, why are gubernatorial elections held in off years?
   A. so that gubernatorial elections will not be influenced by a presidential election
   B. so that candidates cannot run for governor and a federal office at the same time
   C. so that voters will not become overwhelmed by too many candidates in one year
   D. because Texas happened to became part of the United States during an off year

   A (p. 945)

6. What is the ultimate check on an elected official in Texas?
   A. impeachment
   B. the Sunset review process
   C. the budgetary review process
   D. campaign donations

   A (p. 946)

7. In Texas, if a sitting governor is unable to hold office, due to impeachment and conviction, resignation, or death, who becomes governor?
   A. the secretary of state
   B. the lieutenant governor
   C. the Speaker of the state House of Representatives
   D. The Texas constitution requires the lieutenant governor to appoint a temporary replacement until an election can be held.

   B (p. 947)

8. What is the most important and far-reaching of the Texas governor's powers?
   A. the power to appoint boards and commissions
   B. the power to call special sessions
   C. the power to submit a budget to the legislature
   D. the line-item veto

   A (p. 948)

9. What is the most important function of the Texas governor's staff?
   A. to keep the governor informed about problems and issues

    B. to act as lobbyists for the governor's agenda in the legislature
    C. to represent the governor's office in different parts of the state
    D. to organize the governor's electoral campaigns

    A (p. 948)

10. Which of the following is the best example of the Texas governor's exercise of senatorial courtesy?
    A. The governor will not appoint someone to office unless that appointee's state senator agrees.
    B. The governor will not veto a bill without first giving the bill's senate sponsor an opportunity to amend it.
    C. The Senate will use the governor's budget plan as its blueprint for the upcoming session.
    D. The governor will address the full Senate at the beginning of each legislative session.

    A (p. 949)

11. Which of the following is the best example of the Texas governor's military powers?
    A. The governor can declare martial law during a natural disaster.
    B. The governor can use federal troops stationed in camps within Texas.
    C. All governors receive a National Guard pension when they retire.
    D. All governors automatically possess the rank of general in the U.S. Armed Forces.

    A (p. 950)

12. When the Texas governor strikes out particular spending provisions in an appropriations bill, this is called
    A. a line-item veto.
    B. a postadjournment veto.
    C. a pocket veto.
    D. an unconstitutional action.

    A (p. 950)

13. What is the Texas governor's greatest judicial power?
    A. the power to appoint, with the Senate's consent, judges to appeals courts
    B. the power to appoint judges to vacancies on the courts
    C. the power to restrict the types of cases the appeals courts may decide
    D. the power to remove judges

    B (p. 953)

14. Which of the following was a powerful three-term governor who presided over Texas during the 1960s?
    A. John Connally
    B. Dolph Briscoe
    C. W. Lee "Pappy" O'Daniel
    D. Coke Stevenson

    A (p. 954)

15. In Texas, who is the one officer in the plural executive who is NOT elected by voters?
    A. the secretary of state
    B. the attorney general
    C. the comptroller
    D. the lieutenant governor

    A (p. 955)

16. What is the primary task of the Texas secretary of state?
    A. to oversee the state's foreign, economic, and diplomatic policy
    B. to handle elections and voter registration
    C. to collect child support payments
    D. to coordinate and plan projects in conjunction with the federal government

    B (p. 956)

17. The chief lawyer for Texas is
    A. the chief justice of the state supreme court.
    B. the attorney general.
    C. the secretary of state.
    D. the state comptroller.

    B (p. 958)

18. The Texas governor has all of the following legislative powers EXCEPT
    A. the power to address the legislature in state of the state speeches.
    B. the power to sign and veto bills.
    C. the power to call special sessions.
    D. the power to break tie votes in the Senate.

    D (pp. 951–53)

19. Which of the following about the lieutenant governor in Texas is INCORRECT?
    A. The lieutenant governor is a full member of the Texas Senate.
    B. The lieutenant governor presides over the Senate.
    C. The lieutenant governor is elected in a statewide election.
    D. The lieutenant governor's powers are primarily legislative, not executive.

    A (p. 956)

20. Who has NEVER been a lieutenant governor in Texas?
    A. Bob Bullock
    B. Rodney Ellis
    C. Rick Perry
    D. Bill Ratliff

    B (pp. 956–57)

21. In Texas, what is the most important power of the state comptroller?
    A. estimating the tax revenues for the legislature
    B. overseeing the state police and the Texas Rangers
    C. enforcing all state land use and takings laws
    D. regulating the oil industry in the state

    A (p. 961)

22. In Texas, the plural executive is directly accountable to the legislature through
    A. the budgetary process.
    B. Sunset review.
    C. the impeachment process.
    D. All of the above.

    D (p. 962)

23. Which of the following is NOT one of the tasks of the Texas Ethics Commission?
    A. It administers and enforces election codes concerning political contributions.
    B. It monitors the activities of lobbyists.
    C. It offers advisory opinions on the propriety of actions taken by public officials.
    D. It handles the initial investigation of all public officials charged with impeachable offenses.

    D (pp. 968–69)

24. What has been a major criticism brought against the Texas State Commission on Judicial Conduct?
    A. The commission's officers have been guilty of accepting bribes from judges and lawyers.
    B. The commission's members are not elected and thus are not publicly accountable.
    C. There is a lack of openness in the commission's disciplinary hearings.
    D. There should be no review of judges' behavior except for an impeachment hearing.

    C (p. 970)

25. What is the purpose of the Sunset Advisory Commission in Texas?
    A. It reviews state agencies every twelve years to see if they are still needed.
    B. It administers state programs for the elderly.
    C. It oversees the retirement of state bureaucratic workers.
    D. It runs the Texas Chamber of Commerce.

    A (p. 971)

TRUE OR FALSE

1. The Texas governor has many formal powers, making him or her one of the United States's strongest chief executives.

   F (p. 943)

2. Texas has a plural executive made up of multiple popularly elected offices.

   T (p. 943)

3. George W. Bush was the first Republican governor of Texas since Reconstruction.

   F (p. 944)

4. The governor of Texas currently serves a two-year term in office.

   F (p. 945)

5. The governor makes approximately three thousand appointments to executive boards and commissions during a single term in office.

   T (p. 948)

6. Both the lieutenant governor and the secretary of state in Texas have the authority to call a special session of the legislature.

   F (p. 953)

7. The attorney general in Texas is responsible for overseeing the registration of voters.

   F (p. 956)

8. The lieutenant governor in Texas is also the president of the Senate and may cast a vote to break a tie.

   T (p. 956)

9. Most members of state boards and commissions in Texas are elected for six-year terms.

   F (p. 963)

10. The Texas Sunset Advisory Commission has mandated that no government official may serve in any single office for more than twelve years.

    F (p. 972)

CHAPTER 25 | The Texas Judiciary

MULTIPLE CHOICE

1. What types of cases does the Texas Supreme Court hear?
   A. civil and juvenile appeals
   B. appeals on civil and criminal cases
   C. both trial and appeals in tort law cases
   D. final appeals on all civil and death penalty cases

   A (p. 978)

2. The main trial courts in Texas are called
   A. county courts.
   B. courts of appeals.
   C. district courts.
   D. municipal courts.

   C (p. 980)

3. Which court in Texas has automatic jurisdiction over all death penalty cases?
   A. the Court of Criminal Appeals
   B. the Supreme Court
   C. district court
   D. the justice of the peace court

   A (p. 980)

4. Which of the following statements best describes the structure of the Texas judiciary?
   A. It is a system designed to favor the plaintiffs in economic disputes.
   B. It is a compact and highly centralized system.
   C. It is a system that is very dependent on the executive branch.
   D. It is very decentralized, designed to provide local justice.

   D (p. 980)

5. Disputes between private individuals over their relationships, responsibilities, and obligations are the topic of
   A. criminal law.
   B. civil law.
   C. statutory law.
   D. ordinances.

   B (p. 982)

6. Justice of the peace courts handle what kind of disputes?
   A. small claims
   B. felonies
   C. city ordinance violations
   D. All of the above.

   A (p. 981)

7. If you violate a city ordinance, what type of court would most likely hear your case?
   A. a district court
   B. a municipal court
   C. a county court
   D. a court of appeal

   B (p. 981)

8. What is the standard of proof used for civil cases in Texas?
   A. The defendant must be found guilty beyond a reasonable doubt.
   B. The plaintiff must meet the preponderance of evidence.
   C. The defendant must prove a reasonable chance of innocence.
   D. The defendant must have contributed a higher campaign donation to the judge's campaign than the plaintiff.

   B (p. 982)

9. The most common route to a criminal conviction is
   A. a bench trial.
   B. a jury trial.

C. a plea bargain between the defendant and the state.
D. an indictment from a grand jury.

C (p. 984)

10. Trial lawyers tend to support
    A. Democratic judicial candidates.
    B. Republican judicial candidates.
    C. anti–death penalty judicial candidates.
    D. probusiness judicial candidates.

    A (p. 985)

11. What is the most important role the governor of Texas plays in the judicial process?
    A. The governor has the power to permanently appoint all municipal court judges.
    B. The governor has the power to limit the jurisdiction of the appellate courts.
    C. The governor has the power to appoint judges to fill any vacancies on the bench for the time period before elections are held.
    D. The governor has the power to add additional judges to the appellate courts whenever there is a six-month backlog in cases.

    C (p. 986)

12. Why does it typically cost more money to win a seat on the Texas Supreme Court than a seat on the Court of Criminal Appeals?
    A. The Texas legislature has placed a strict cap on the spending for the Criminal Appeals Court election campaigns.
    B. There are few interest groups that contribute money to the Criminal Appeals Court candidates' campaign, which keeps the costs of the election down.
    C. Judges running for the Criminal Appeals Court do not have to be elected in a statewide election.
    D. Fewer people are interested in the Court of Criminal Appeals.

    B (pp. 985–87)

13. What is the most important part of a judicial candidate's campaign in Texas?
    A. party affiliation
    B. professional and personal qualifications
    C. name recognition with the voters
    D. rating by the American Bar Association

    A (p. 987)

14. What is the particular problem in judicial elections called the "name game"?
    A. Voters will often vote for a candidate by looking at her or his party affiliation, not their name.
    B. Many voters will vote for a judicial candidate with a name they are familiar with, even if they know nothing about the candidate.
    C. Judicial candidates sometimes make up colorful nicknames, like "Hang 'Em High" Johnson, that serve as free advertisements for their judging beliefs.
    D. Only big-name candidates can raise enough campaign contributions.

    B (p. 990)

15. What is the major criticism of the method of judicial selection in Texas today?
    A. It is overly partisan.
    B. The need to raise campaign contributions compromises the independence of the judges.
    C. Too often voters know nothing about the judicial candidates for whom they are to vote.
    D. All of the above.

    D (pp. 987–93)

16. Approximately what percentage of Texas judges are women?
    A. under 5 percent
    B. between 10 and 20 percent
    C. between 25 and 35 percent
    D. approximately 50 percent

    C (p. 994)

17. What is the reason that there are few minority judges in Texas?
    A. One must be a lawyer to be a judge, and there are few minority lawyers in Texas.
    B. Judicial districts are often quite large, and minority voters rarely make up a majority in these districts.
    C. Minority voters tend to be Democrats and the Republican Party dominates Texas elections.
    D. All of the above.

    D (p. 994)

18. What is it called when a blue ribbon committee selects judicial nominees who are then appointed by the governor and must finally run for retention in office?
    A. *en blanc* selection
    B. progressive reform selection

C. nonpartisan selection
D. merit selection

D (p. 997)

19. The Texas Judicial Campaign Fairness Act
    A. limits the amount of campaign contributions a judicial candidate can receive from an individual donor.
    B. compels judges to recuse themselves from any case involving someone who has contributed money to their campaign.
    C. restricts judicial advertising to radio and television ads.
    D. forbids law firms or corporations from making donations.

A (p. 998)

20. Which of the following explains why Texas has one of the most controversial death penalty systems in the United States?
    A. Almost no death penalty case has been overturned by the Court of Criminal Appeals.
    B. The court-appointed lawyers the state provides defendants have often been subpar.
    C. There are racial and ethnic disparities in who receives the death penalty and who does not.
    D. All of the above.

D (pp. 1001–1002)

21. What is the process for granting clemency in Texas?
    A. The governor has complete control of whether to grant clemency.
    B. The governor must follow the recommendations of the Texas Board of Pardons and Paroles.
    C. The Texas Board of Pardons and Paroles makes a unilateral collective decision.
    D. There is no procedure for clemency in Texas.

B (p. 1002)

22. Which of the following best describes the incarceration rate in Texas, compared with that in other states?
    A. Texas has a lower-than-average rate of incarceration.
    B. The Texas incarceration rate is about the national average.
    C. Texas is in the top one-third of states in terms of the percentage of population in prison.
    D. Texas's incarceration rate is among the top three state incarceration rates.

D (p. 1002)

23. Which of the following best describes capital punishment in Texas?
    A. The number of prisoners executed in Texas has been slowly decreasing since the 1970s.
    B. Texas has both the highest rate of executions and the highest rate of successful death sentence appeals in the nation.
    C. Texas executes more individuals than any other state and has a statistically low rate of successfully appealed capital cases.
    D. The number of executions in Texas is double the number of executions in every other state combined.

    C (p. 1001)

24. Since the late 1980s, in what direction has the Texas Supreme Court moved, regarding civil cases?
    A. The Texas Supreme Court has grown more liberal in its tort law decisions.
    B. Texas has moved toward a more common law approach to torts.
    C. The Texas Supreme Court has taken a more pro-business direction.
    D. The Texas Supreme Court is moving toward a more common law approach to tort reform.

    C (p. 1004)

25. What is the most important type of case that the Texas Supreme Court handles?
    A. impeachment of public officials
    B. tort laws
    C. prison reform
    D. death penalty cases

    B (p. 1003)

TRUE OR FALSE

1. Texas followed the pattern of the U.S. judiciary by dividing the top appellate court into two separate courts, each with different jurisdictions.

   F (p. 978)

2. Texan justices of the peace do not have to be lawyers.

   T (p. 981)

3. Plea bargains are not often used in Texas criminal trials.

   F (p. 984)

4. In Texas, appellate court judges are elected but trial judges are appointed by the governor to six-year terms.

    F (p. 985)

5. Judicial elections in Texas are nonpartisan.

    F (p. 987)

6. One of the biggest controversies concerning the method of judicial selection in Texas is that there may be conflicts of interest when judges must hear cases determining the financial interests of persons who have donated to their campaign.

    T (p. 987)

7. The most critical factor in winning any judicial election in Texas is to be affiliated with the Democratic Party.

    F (p. 987)

8. Fewer than 15 percent of all judges in Texas are Hispanic.

    T (p. 993)

9. Texas leads the nation in the number of state-sanctioned executions.

    T (p. 1001)

10. The governor of Texas is unable to grant clemency to death row inmates without the recommendation of the Texas Board of Pardons and Paroles.

    T (p. 1002)

CHAPTER 26 | Local Government in Texas

MULTIPLE CHOICE

1. Why are Texas counties important?
   A. They create and regulate cities.
   B. They act as a legislative body, making most of the local laws.
   C. They provide the main form of government in rural areas.
   D. All of the above.

   C (p. 1013)

2. In Texas, what is the name of the officer who presides over the county commissioners' court?
   A. county judge
   B. executive commissioner
   C. justice of the peace
   D. sheriff

   A (p. 1013)

3. Which of the following is NOT a function of county government in Texas?
   A. supervising road and bridge maintenance
   B. administering water districts
   C. setting a county's tax rates
   D. maintaining the county jail

   B (pp. 1014–15)

4. Which of the following statements about counties in Texas is INCORRECT?
   A. Counties are an administrative arm of state governments.
   B. There are over 250 counties in Texas.
   C. Each county has four county commissioners.

276

D. All counties have approximately the same number of people.

D (pp. 1013–14)

5. What is a key problem with counties in Texas?
   A. Many of them are too small and underpopulated to function well.
   B. County laws were made in the nineteenth century, making them too old-fashioned.
   C. They have not been given adequate lawmaking powers by the legislature.
   D. Too often the county seats cannot be reached in a day's drive.

   A (p. 1020)

6. What is the main difference between a home rule city and a general law city?
   A. A general law city does not have a mayor.
   B. A general law city is chartered for localities with a population of less than 5,000 persons.
   C. A general law city is the name for all cities incorporated after 1901.
   D. A general law city has no power to set the property tax.

   B (p. 1022)

7. A home rule charter
   A. grants a city a great deal of autonomy.
   B. sets limits to how much property tax the city may levy.
   C. can more easily borrow money than general law cities.
   D. All of the above.

   D (p. 1022)

8. The commissioner form of city government was developed as a response to
   A. the end of Reconstruction in 1876.
   B. the hurricane at Galveston in 1900.
   C. the Great Depression of 1929.
   D. the discovery of oil in 1901.

   B (p. 1025)

9. What is the level of popularity of the commissioner system of city government in Texas today?
   A. It is the most popular form of city government in Texas.
   B. No city in Texas today has a pure commissioner system, but a handful claim a variation of the system.
   C. While less popular than the mayor-council system, over 100 cities in Texas today use the commissioner style.
   D. Commissioner systems have never been used in Texas.

   B (p. 1026)

10. What is an at-large election?
    A. an election for offices that receive no official salary
    B. an election in which voters elect officials from the entire geographical area, rather than from a smaller district within the area
    C. an election held under the commission system of city government
    D. an election in which one or more candidates are under criminal indictment

    B (p. 1026)

11. Which of the following is NOT a key difference between the mayor-council and the council-manager forms of local government?
    A. The council-manager style was meant to reduce the possibility of corruption that the mayor-council system may bring.
    B. The council-manager system is the most popular form of government throughout the United States for cities of over 10,000 residents.
    C. In the council-manager system, the chief executive is a city manager, not a mayor.
    D. In the council-manager system, local politics is viewed as a full-time job, unlike in the mayor-council system.

    D (p. 1026)

12. What was the effect of Dallas's shifting from an at-large to a single-member district system in 1991?
    A. The change was responsible for the election of a significant number of African American and Hispanic council members.
    B. The city lost its status as a home rule city for five years.
    C. At-large districts benefited the local Republican Party.
    D. It was challenged in court but found constitutional by the Texas Supreme Court.

    A (p. 1027)

13. San Antonio operates under what form of city government?
    A. mayor-council style
    B. council-manager style
    C. commissioner style
    D. at-large style

    B (p. 1028)

14. Which of the following cities currently has a city government with a strong mayor form of government?
    A. Dallas
    B. San Antonio

C. Austin
D. Houston

D (p. 1027)

15. The chief financial officer for a city is called the
    A. city controller.
    B. sheriff.
    C. mayor.
    D. city manager.

    A (p. 1027)

16. Which of the following is the most common form of local government in Texas?
    A. county government
    B. municipal government
    C. special districts
    D. None of the above.

    C (p. 1029)

17. A school district is
    A. a special district.
    B. administered by the county commissioners' court.
    C. ruled by the state government in Austin.
    D. established by each incorporated city.

    A (p. 1029)

18. What is the main difference between a special district and a county?
    A. A special district provides only one specific service within a geographic region.
    B. A county is formed in terms of population density, while a special district is created geographically.
    C. Special districts are controlled by incorporated cities, unlike county government.
    D. There are no major differences.

    A (p. 1029)

19. Which of the following is NOT a service that is provided by a special district?
    A. hospital
    B. school
    C. electricity
    D. city police

    D (p. 1029)

280 | Chapter 26

20. In Texas, who creates special districts?
    A. the Texas legislature
    B. the governor
    C. Texas voters in the areas that will be covered
    D. the county commissioners' court, with local voter approval

    C (p. 1031)

21. How are most special districts in Texas administered?
    A. County judges administer all special districts within their jurisdiction.
    B. They are run by a board, elected by residents within the district.
    C. For each special district, the governor appoints members to a review board.
    D. They are run by special district administers who answer directly to the state legislature.

    B (p. 1031)

22. What are the main sources of revenue for special districts in Texas?
    A. property taxes and user fees
    B. income tax and user fees
    C. income taxes and sales tax
    D. sales tax and property tax

    A (p. 1031)

23. What type of government is often called hidden government because people often don't know it exists?
    A. county government
    B. special districts
    C. city government
    D. state government

    B (p. 1031)

24. What is the function of the twenty-four councils of government in Texas today?
    A. They are a board that establishes new special districts when needed.
    B. They are a regional board meant to coordinate local planning and economic development.
    C. They are a tax board meant to establish local property tax rates.
    D. They are an administrative board that runs utility districts in rural areas.

    B (p. 1033)

25. Which of the following has been a problem in the system of special districts found recently in Texas?
    A. State investigations have discovered numerous "phantom districts" that do not provide a service, yet bill the local counties for administrative costs.

B. Real estate developers have moved a few people onto land rent free, who then vote for huge bond measures that future residents are obliged to pay.
C. The special districts for homeland security throughout Texas were uncoordinated and ill prepared for 9/11.
D. All of the above.

B (pp. 1032–33)

TRUE OR FALSE

1. County governments are most important for administering rural areas throughout Texas.

   T (p. 1013)

2. The chief executive officer of each county in Texas is the sheriff.

   F (p. 1014)

3. Each county in Texas is required by the state constitution to have approximately the same number of residents.

   F (p. 1016)

4. General law cities have more autonomy from the state than home-rule-chartered cities.

   F (p. 1022)

5. Commissioner governments are designed to run school districts and other special districts throughout the state.

   F (p. 1024)

6. All large cities in Texas have structures of government that give strong executive powers to the mayor.

   F (p. 1025)

7. San Antonio and Dallas both have council-manager forms of government.

   T (p. 1025)

8. Special districts are the most common form of government in Texas.

   T (p. 1029)

9. In Texas, special districts are run by a board of trustees appointed by the governor.

   F (p. 1031)

10. One of the problems with Texas government is that there are no regional councils that promote coordinated planning across local governments.

    F (p. 1033)

CHAPTER 27 | Public Policy in Texas

MULTIPLE CHOICE

1. What is the result of Texas's status as a low-tax state?
   A. Texas is often in debt.
   B. Texas offers fewer services.
   C. Texas requires a higher level of federal matching funds than other states.
   D. Texas will need the income tax in the near future.

   B (p. 1040)

2. Which form of taxation is not used in Texas?
   A. income tax
   B. property tax
   C. oil production tax
   D. sales tax

   A (p. 1040)

3. Which of the following is the best definition of a dedicated fund?
   A. money that is given to a state or local government through citizens donating extra tax dollars, designed for specific projects
   B. the type of funding that requires a state agency to make biannual budget forecasts, rather than just one a year
   C. spending priorities that are beneficial to specific interest groups, which always have groups of politicians backing them
   D. portions of the state budget that are mandated to be spent in specific ways, like for Medicaid payments

   D (p. 1042)

4. Why do Texas budgets not run into debt?
   A. The oil booms of the last century always provided plenty of income.
   B. The Texas constitution places several limitations on the ability of the legislature to get into debt.
   C. The political ideology of Texas has always made borrowing money politically unpopular.
   D. The tax levels have always been among the highest in the nation, so there is plenty of money available.

   B (p. 1042)

5. What limits does the Texas constitution place on welfare spending?
   A. No more than 1 percent of the budget may be used for welfare spending.
   B. The ratio of federal dollars to state dollars must be set at no less than 4 to 1.
   C. Legislature cannot appropriate more than 10 percent of the budget on welfare.
   D. All welfare spending must be paid for through property taxes, with tax levels set by each county.

   A (p. 1042)

6. What are the two most important agencies or offices responsible for preparing the Texas state budget?
   A. the legislative budget board and the comptroller
   B. the House appropriations committee and the Senate finance committee
   C. the governor and the Senate finance committee
   D. the Speaker of the House and the governor

   A (p. 1043)

7. Sales and use taxes in Texas have led some to complain that the tax system in Texas is too
   A. complex.
   B. onerous.
   C. progressive.
   D. regressive.

   D (p. 1047)

8. Which of the following poses the greatest threat to Texas's dependence on sales tax?
   A. the decline in consumer spending
   B. the decline in the number of companies moving to Texas
   C. e-commerce
   D. None of the above.

   C (p. 1049)

9. What is the greatest source of revenue for Texas?
   A. taxes
   B. federal matching funds
   C. licenses and fees
   D. tobacco company settlement money

   A (p. 1049)

10. Which programs in Texas receive the largest amount of federal matching funds to supplement state tax dollars?
    A. education
    B. transportation
    C. health and human services
    D. public housing

    C (p. 1049)

11. What was the effect on Texas prisons of the Supreme Court case *Ruiz v. Estelle*?
    A. Texas was compelled to suspend the death penalty during the 1980s.
    B. Texas's prison system was declared unconstitutional, and the federal courts stepped in to oversee its administration.
    C. The Texas policy of leasing prisoners as workers to private companies was declared unconstitutional.
    D. Death by hanging was declared constitutional.

    B (p. 1054)

12. On which budget item does Texas spend the most money?
    A. transportation
    B. education
    C. heath and human services
    D. corrections programs and prison maintenance

    B (p. 1051)

13. The policy on criminal offenders in Texas favors
    A. rehabilitation programs.
    B. imprisonment of only violent offenders.
    C. imprisonment of violent and nonviolent offenders.
    D. using early pardons and suspended sentences to reduce the prison population.

    C (p. 1059)

14. What has been the main result of the "get tough on crime" policy in Texas?
    A. The number of prison inmates in Texas has risen.
    B. There has been a continuous need for more prisons.

    C. The cost of prison construction in Texas has risen.
    D. All of the above.

    D (p. 1059)

15. What was Texas's response to the federal government's order to desegregate schools in the 1950s?
    A. Texas launched an immediate, statewide resistance to desegregation.
    B. Some school districts quickly desegregated, while others resisted integration well into the 1960s.
    C. Unlike much of the Deep South, Texas integrated its schools with little trouble.
    D. Texas school districts had never been legally segregated.

    B (p. 1061)

16. Which of the following is the best description of the Supreme Court's decision in *Rodriguez v. San Antonio ISD*?
    A. The state may not deny federal education dollars to underperforming school districts.
    B. The Equal Protection Clause of the Fourteenth Amendment compels states to fund all school districts equally.
    C. Segregation based on a student's ethnicity is unconstitutional.
    D. It is not unconstitutional for Texas to fund school districts with unequal levels of property taxes.

    D (p. 1062)

17. In what case did the Texas Supreme Court declare that the Texas constitution required that each school district be funded at approximately the same level?
    A. *Edgewood IDS v. Kirby*
    B. *Brown v. Board of Education*
    C. *Rodriguez v. San Antonio IDS*
    D. *Ruiz v. Estelle*

    A (pp. 1062–63)

18. As it pertains to Texas, what is the Robin Hood policy?
    A. a law that demands that anyone found guilty of a property crime of over $1,000 must spend at least five years in jail
    B. a program designed to equalize school funding by transferring funds from wealthy to poor schools
    C. a new state welfare policy that imposed a tax on all businesses that lay off more than ten workers
    D. None of the above.

    B (p. 1064)

19. During the 1980s, what controversial policy did the education committee SCOPE, headed by Ross Perot, recommend?
    A. a "no pass, no play" policy for student athletes
    B. the equity-in-school-funding plan, known as Robin Hood
    C. quicker desegregation of the schools
    D. more decentralization in school administration

    A (p. 1065)

20. How have education reforms in Texas in the 1990s differed from those in the 1980s?
    A. Reforms in the 1990s cut education spending, compared with the 1980s.
    B. Reforms in the 1990s further centralized school administration at the state level.
    C. Reforms in the 1990s gave back more autonomy to local school districts.
    D. Reforms in the 1980s emphasized more bilingual education than those in the 1990s.

    C (p. 1066)

21. Which of the following demographic groups is statistically most likely to live below the poverty level?
    A. two-parent households with over five children when both parents have low levels of education
    B. families headed by single mothers
    C. the elderly
    D. single unemployed men

    B (p. 1068)

22. Where in Texas are the poverty levels at their highest?
    A. in the Gulf region
    B. in the north central region of Dallas–Fort Worth
    C. in South and West Texas
    D. in the Panhandle

    C (p. 1068)

23. In the mid-1990s, growing discontent over welfare policy across the country encouraged many states, including Texas, to seek _____ so that they could experiment with welfare reform.
    A. block grants
    B. grants-in-aid
    C. preemption
    D. waivers

    D (p. 1073)

Public Policy in Texas | 287

24. When the Texas legislature voted on welfare reform in 1995, the result was
    A. narrow passage in both the House and Senate, with the support coming only from Republicans.
    B. overwhelming bipartisan support in the both the House and the Senate.
    C. rejection after a long and acrimonious debate in the House.
    D. immediate rejection after little debate in both the House and the Senate.

    B (p. 1073)

25. What is the best explanation for the drop in the number of Texans on welfare in the late 1990s?
    A. the success of the welfare reforms of 1996
    B. the booming economy and the rising demand for all types of labor
    C. the reduction in the state's definition of poverty
    D. There has actually been a rise in the number of welfare recipients in Texas.

    B (p. 1075)

TRUE OR FALSE

1. The state constitution requires that Texas maintain a balanced budget.

    T (p. 1042)

2. The tax on oil and natural gas is the most important source of revenue for Texas government.

    F (p. 1044)

3. Many commentators have argued that the Texas tax system is regressive, falling more heavily on the poor.

    T (p. 1047)

4. The largest expense in the Texas budget is transportation costs.

    F (p. 1051)

5. Texas has one of the lowest rates of incarceration in the nation.

    F (p. 1057)

6. The Robin Hood plan is a controversial program of transferring funds from wealthier schools to poorer schools, to equalize funding.

    T (p. 1064)

7. School reform in the 1990s led to the centralization of education policy in Austin.

   F (p. 1066)

8. Texas is in the bottom third of states in the rate of high school graduation.

   T (p. 1067)

9. Almost 50 percent of families below the poverty line in Texas are headed by a single mother.

   T (p. 1068)

10. The 1990s saw an increase in the number of persons on welfare in Texas.

    F (p. 1075)